101
WAYS TO
REACH YOUR
COMMUNITY

STEVE SJOGREN

NAVPRESS
BRINGING TRUTH TO LIFE
P.O. Box 35001, Colorado Springs, Colorado 80935

OUR GUARANTEE TO YOU

We believe so strongly in the message of our books that we are making this quality guarantee to you. If for any reason you are disappointed with the content of this book, return the title page to us with your name and address and we will refund to you the list price of the book. To help us serve you better, please briefly describe why you were disappointed. Mail your refund request to: NavPress, P.O. Box 35002, Colorado Springs, CO 80935.

The Navigators is an international Christian organization. Our mission is to reach, disciple, and equip people to know Christ and to make Him known through successive generations. We envision multitudes of diverse people in the United States and every other nation who have a passionate love for Christ, live a lifestyle of sharing Christ's love, and multiply spiritual laborers among those without Christ.

NavPress is the publishing ministry of The Navigators. NavPress publications help believers learn biblical truth and apply what they learn to their lives and ministries. Our mission is to stimulate spiritual formation among our readers.

Library of Congress Catalog Card Number: 00-061683
ISBN 1-57683-220-1

Cover design by Jennifer Mahalik
Cover photos by Adobe Image Library
Creative Team: Brad Lewis, Amy Spencer, Heather Nordyke

Some of the anecdotal illustrations in this book are true to life and are included with the permission of the persons involved. All other illustrations are composites of real situations, and any resemblance to people living or dead is coincidental.

Unless otherwise identified, all Scripture quotations in this publication are taken from the *Holy Bible: New International Version®* (NIV®). Copyright © 1973, 1978, 1984 by International Bible Society. Used by permission of Zondervan Publishing House. All rights reserved. Another version used is the *New American Standard Bible* (NASB), © The Lockman Foundation 1960, 1962, 1963, 1968, 1971, 1972, 1973, 1975, 1977.

Sjogren, Steve, 1955-
    101 ways to reach your community / by Steve Sjogren.
        p. cm.
    ISBN 1-57683-220-1 (pbk.)
    1. Evangelistic work. 2. Service (Theology) I. Title: One hundred one ways to reach your community. II. Title: One hundred and one ways to reach your community. III. Title.

BV3770 .S53 2001
269'.2—dc21
                                                                        00-061683

Printed in the United States of America

3 4 5 6 7 8 9 10 / 05 04 03 02 01

CONTENTS

103401

LEVEL 2: CONNECTING TO THE COMMUNITY

Level 3: Investing in the City

INTRODUCTION

As a child I was intrigued by cookbooks. I enjoyed paging through them to see what could be done when a few simple kitchen elements were mixed together and cooked properly. Even as an eight-year-old, I took on some pretty ambitious cooking projects. Usually, the cookbook picture looked a lot nicer than my finished product, but the practice was exciting just the same. I always had fun. No matter how the dish turned out, I gained confidence as a chef in progress.

AN OUTREACH COOKBOOK

Think of this book as an interactive cookbook. The concepts outlined here are designed to be first read and then done by you with a few friends, with your small group, or perhaps with your entire church. This is a read-and-do book. If you only *read* this book, you'll miss the point. That would be the equivalent of seeing a photo of a dish in a cookbook, saying, "I like that dish," then eating the picture! So first you should *read,* then *do* these projects. The concepts in this book won't make sense unless you live them out.

I encourage you to take this book along as you cook up each outreach. In fact, get it dirty! Wear it out! Let's make some forward progress for God's kingdom.

LET'S CHANGE THE WORLD!

AL

In a heartfelt note to me, Al described himself as a "former highly driven, money-motivated entrepreneur." He usually worked sixty hours a week at his consulting business. Though he was raised attending church, he says he "evaporated" shortly after his first communion service as a teenager. And while he had possessed a childhood faith, he had long since forgotten God by the time he got into his late thirties. Looking back now, he says, his spiritual condition was as cold as the blustery winter night when he ran into some people from our church doing a coffee outreach.

Along with several hundred other moviegoers, Al was waiting in a long line on the opening night of a popular movie. The frigid weather made the wait downright painful. To his surprise, a number of people were making their way through the crowd offering hot drinks to the movie fans as the line snaked its way into the theater. He was more curious about these people than just the free drinks they were offering. When they came up to him, they offered him a hot chocolate or coffee to show him "God's love in a practical way." He said no thanks to the drink but took the card, which had information with the church's name, phone number, and location. His skepticism came out immediately: "Oh, I get it, you're doing this so I'll come to your church, right?" He wasn't ready for their response.

"We'd be thrilled if you came to our church, but no, we're not doing this for that reason. We're here because it's cold and you look like you could use some warmth! Besides that, God really loves you!" He could have fended off about any other response than that. He said he was so moved by their compassion, authenticity, and dedication that he could scarcely enjoy the movie! He did come to church the following weekend and the weekend after that and so on. It's been three years since that winter night, and Al has not only come to Christ, he also has grown immensely in his Christian life. He is now one of our most prolific leaders in reaching out with servant evangelism. In fact, he travels to other cities to teach churches how to do servant evangelism!

CHUCK

Chuck was an alcoholic for years. Like many veterans of Alcoholics Anonymous (AA), he had an experience with his "Higher Power" and thankfully stopped drinking. "But there is a difference," he says, "between stopping the negative patterns and filling yourself with something positive. I was no longer drinking, but I was empty inside."

An outreach team from my church met Chuck one Saturday afternoon at a soft drink outreach. As he came into the stadium, like hundreds of other fans he received a drink with a small card that read, "You looked too thirsty to pass up! If we can be of more help to you, please give us a call." A few weeks later Chuck used the card as a map and made his way to church. Within a month of hearing about the love of God he decided to take the plunge—he received Jesus. That inner emptiness began to be filled with the presence of Christ.

Not long after coming to our church, Chuck heard about servant evangelism outreach opportunities. One of the principles from AA that he had never really worked on was "You get better as you serve others." He told me, "I don't know if I can do this stuff. I'm not much of a talker."

I encouraged him: "Why don't you come and just carry things at first. We'll take it a step at a time." So Chuck began to attend our Saturday outreaches faithfully and to carry what we were using in our outreach projects. Over the past six months he's gotten more confident. On a recent Saturday morning I asked him, "Are you still having fun?" I loved his response:

"Now I'm *showing* and *telling* people about the love of Christ."

BILL

I met Bill at the mall at our church's Christmas gift-wrapping outreach. He was the leader of the crew of twelve. I'd never really talked with him before, so to break the ice I asked, "How did you find your way into our church?" He explained that the church had literally come to him a couple of years back while he was busy at the engineering firm where he works. An outreach team met Bill one day as they were doing a restroom cleaning project. He was a bit taken aback when they offered their introduction: "Hi, we'd like to clean your toilets for free—just to show you the love of Christ."

"That's kind of a polarizing opener," Chuck says. "You tend to either laugh, thinking this must be a joke, or you just recoil in shock. Personally, I was totally surprised by the offer."

He was so moved by the project that he decided to check out

what kind of church would clean toilets. The minute he walked into our church, he connected with what we're all about.

"I had always had a concept of God, but it was kind of vague," Chuck says. "Your outreach got me hooked enough to come and check out what was going on. I received Christ, and my life has changed in some amazing ways since then. I mean, look at me— I'm helping lead the charge now by wrapping presents at the mall. I know it doesn't take an engineer to wrap presents, so hey, I get the job done."

YEAH, BUT CAN ANYONE DO IT?

Al, Chuck, and Bill have all come to Christ through a simple approach to outreach called servant evangelism. This is an approach to sharing Christ that anyone with a heart of availability to God can do.

I didn't always think of evangelism as such a doable task. As a new Christian I was highly motivated to see my friends and family come to Christ. I was madly in love with Jesus, and more than anything in the world I wanted everyone else to have that same love in their hearts.

Though I had a great heart motivation, at times my methods left a lot to be desired. I was willing to try any evangelistic approach at least once. As I look back now I shudder at some of the shenanigans I pulled. Don't get me wrong—I'm all for any approach that will get the good news out to people, but I went a bit overboard at times. For example, when invited to a friend's house for dinner, sometime during the evening I'd excuse myself to use the bathroom. Then I'd unroll the toilet paper several feet, place in it a frightening gospel tract, and roll it back up. (I called that a "gospel time bomb"—in about twenty-four hours, *boom!* they're going to get it!) I'd go to restaurants and stuff all the menus with tracts. For years, anyone who got a Christmas present from me was sure to receive some sort of study Bible as a gift. (Now I think, *Why would a not-yet-Christian want a study Bible?*)

Anyone who has spent time in the church has probably been exposed to a variety of approaches to evangelism. In my twenty-five years of following Christ, I honestly haven't yet found an approach to evangelism that I don't like. As a pastor, one of my frequently repeated teaching phrases is "Any evangelism is good evangelism." More than anything, it's faithfulness that counts. I think we should be all for any approach to sharing Christ with our lost and sin-entangled world.

However, the older I get as a leader in the body of Christ, the more I ponder the question, "Is what we're doing with evangelism transferable enough that others can also do it?" Effectiveness in accomplishing the goal of leading others to Christ is only part of the equation for consideration. Here's a second, and equally valid, question for all leaders to ponder: "Is what we are doing sustainable by the common follower of Christ?" Far too often, the way we construe evangelism is off-putting—as something only those gifted as evangelists in the body of Christ can pull off.

It was one thing for me to be a little wild in my approach to evangelism, but leading others down a similar path proved to be difficult. A few years into my stint as a pastor, I took an assessment of my leadership effectiveness in the area of evangelism. While I was excited about seeing others come to Christ, I'd never enlisted more than a handful of die-hards in the regular action of evangelism in our church. Try as I did in message after message, I was never able to get more than 1 to 3 percent of my church to be actively involved in evangelism. In my travels to other churches, I find a similar pattern of leadership—pastors who long to see their congregations involved in vital evangelism but who are somehow unable to muster more than a trace of their troops.

So, if there's a desire among pastors and leaders and a commitment of some sort in the hearts of the people, then what's the problem?

SERVANT EVANGELISM: IT'S AN ADJECTIVE THING

A few years ago I began to ask myself, "How can I accomplish a couple of goals: (1) include a much higher percentage of Christians in the action of evangelism, and (2) reach out in significant ways to a lot of people in my city?" As I prayed and pondered and talked with others, it occurred to me that part of the problem was the words I was dealing with.

"Evangelism" is what I call a biblical bipolar word. In other words, it both excites and depresses us when we hear it. It's something we all feel called to do because the love of God compels us and the Word of God commands us to do it. As disciples we are thrilled with the idea of seeing others come to Christ. But on the other hand, we're depressed when it comes to the outworking of that value. We don't have a clue as to how we can realistically pull off that task. So there's a big "Yes, let's do it," but also a big "No, let's not do it the way we've been doing it" going on in our hearts.

I began to experiment some years ago with evangelism projects that were based less on speaking gifts and more on serving gifts. At first, I enlisted a few people and attempted a totally free car wash. Because people are by nature a bit skeptical, the signs read, "Absolutely Free Car Wash!" Those who were served almost insisted on giving us a donation—in spite of our signs. When we refused to receive their donations, those we served were so stunned that they asked, "What's the catch?" We said, "God's love is free, so this gift of service is totally free in the same way."

That first project was so exciting it led to another one the next weekend. Within a month another group of a few guys got the idea that they could expand our serving to include a windshield washing outreach at a local grocery store. This time we were able to touch several hundred with just one small group who masterfully wielded squeegees as they roamed the parking lot. After they cleaned each windshield, they left a card that explained their project.

Those two projects snowballed into a soft drink giveaway, where one team touched several hundred people in just one outreach. I was amazed by this approach we'd stumbled on. After one of our early outreaches, I asked one of my leaders why he thought this was an effective way to do evangelism. I found his response memorable: "It's just two words: Simply effective." To put it another way, by adding the adjective "servant" to the noun "evangelism," the average person was activated.

The adjective "servant" empowers the "common" person in the body of Christ. While only a small percentage of us may picture ourselves as prototypical evangelist types, 100 percent of us have gifts of serving. How do I know that? The Spirit of the Servant dwells inside of us. As we encourage and unleash the gifts of serving present in each believer, and then aim those gifts toward the world, powerful forces for good begin to draw those we serve into a relationship with Christ.

THE NUTS AND BOLTS

EVERY SMALL GROUP OR church needs to have some form of evangelism going on in order to maintain health. But because this can be difficult to pull off, we need to explore some of our motivations for becoming outward people.

Survival: For a group to vitally endure, it must have an explicit outward component. Our church has defined "normal" as one outreach activity every other month. Over the past few years we've learned that this seems to be a reasonable, sustainable balance. Groups that reach out in service will have a healthier atmosphere in the short run and will likely have a much longer life cycle.

Relevance: If we hope to operate in the real world, we must be practically involved in the lives of outsiders who have real problems. The watching world around us will respect our efforts as followers of Christ if our aim goes beyond serving ourselves only.

Fun!: Committed group members will do many things in the name of discipleship and sheer commitment to the cause of Christ, but enjoying themselves is sometimes another question. One of the outreach mantras we often repeat is "A great time was had by all!"

It's tremendously fulfilling to get involved in the life of a community in a practical way. I've found that groups that reach out have no trouble motivating their members to attend group meetings. Why? Because there is a spirit of life in those groups.

Biblical basis: As followers of Jesus, we've all been called to bring the good news to our world (see Matthew 28:18-20). Many Christians experience significant guilt around the topic of evangelism because they know God wants them to tell others about Christ, but they feel a gifting handicap. Be encouraged. You don't have to operate at a phenomenal level of skill to be effective. God isn't looking for heroes with great levels of gifting. Rather, he's looking for available followers who are willing to serve faithfully.

Outwardness: If groups are to be healthy, they need to have an inward-focused component to meet the needs and circumstances of their members. While inwardness is part of the Christian community experience, an outward focus creates balance in the life of a group. Going out is simply healthy and invigorating to the spiritual life of small groups. The good news is that it doesn't take an amazing skill to do significant works of outreach ministry. In fact, it only takes small things—faithful acts of outreach done again and again—to begin to make a difference.

WHAT HAPPENS WHEN WE REACH OUT?

I find Engel's Scale a helpful tool for explaining how someone is progressively led to Christ. Author, teacher, and marketing researcher Jim Engel devised this graph (which I've heavily adapted) to depict the relative level of "lostness" of people before they come to Christ. Someone who is far from beginning a relationship with Christ is at the minus-10 level. As that individual moves forward toward a relationship with Christ through what I call a "nudge of kindness," he or she progresses to a minus-9. Through acts of kindness shown by Christians, conversations they might have with Christian friends, and life traumas (losses in life such as divorce, loss of health, loss of a job), that person progresses toward the positive scale. This trend continues slowly and consistently by the oversight of the Great Spiritual Usher, the Holy Spirit, until that person ultimately comes to Christ.

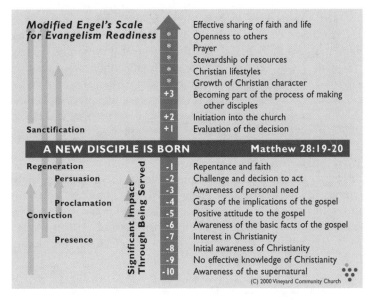

Looking at all the steps in Engel's Scale, the question naturally comes up, "How many 'nudges' does it take for someone to come to Christ?" This is not an exact science, but I believe a pretty close guess, in our day, is it takes between twelve and twenty God-empowered nudges for the average person to come to Christ.

We're Escorting People Forward

Our job isn't to see everyone we encounter come to Christ on the spot. Early in my Christian life I was so enthusiastic about leading others to Christ that I was often overly aggressive with people. The pressure I put on myself was enormous. It was up to me to make something happen.

The movie character I came closest to emotionally was karate king Bruce Lee. His expertise allowed him to grab someone by the hand and, with a quick flick of the wrist, flip him across the room. Before I was introduced to Engel's Scale, I suspect I would have described my job as "to karate flip the unbeliever into full faith in one convincing conversation."

I had no patience for any sort of process of evangelism. But people simply aren't suddenly catapulted into a relationship with Christ. Rather, they take small, progressive, steady steps. The Scriptures say that we are like sheep. Sheep nibble their way from one point to another. If you watch them, they never go anywhere very fast.

The apostle Paul said we are to plant and water seeds (see 1 Corinthians 3:6), but ultimately God is the one who does the harvesting work. Paul also said there is great power unleashed as we plant deeds with the power of Christ's kindness—that this kindness, in fact, leads others to repentance (Romans 2:4). Paul's encouraging view is that there is value in the entire process of evangelism—in the planting, in the watering along the way, and in the final harvesting at the very end of the long process.

We're Answering Their Questions

As we serve people who don't know Christ, they're automatically curious. It's only natural for them to ask, "So, why are you doing this?" In this age of selfishness, it's startling for someone to do a deed of kindness with no apparent strings attached. After we serve, we simply answer the natural questions that come up. I think this is what Peter had in mind when he wrote:

> Always be prepared to give an answer to everyone who asks you
> to give the reason for the hope that you have. (1 Peter 3:15)

I've found that while most Christians don't see themselves as experts in the realm of apologetics (defending the faith), most are able to answer the typical questions that people ask during servant evangelism projects.

We're Loving Them into a Relationship with Christ

There's been a lot of emphasis the last few years on mission statements. Of course I think there's value in focusing the train of attention of an organization. When the church I lead tried to craft a mission statement, we found that we were just too complex in our wording. I believe in simplicity, so we kept working on our mission statement until it became as sleek as possible. It took us a dozen years of thinking, praying, and discussing to boil down our reason for being to the simplest statement possible, but I think we finally got it right:

We exist to love our city into relationship with Jesus Christ.

As I mentioned before, I believe it's the nature of most small groups to move inward upon themselves. I call them "inwardly focused." When we gather, it is only natural to ask each other, "How am I doing? How are you doing? How are we doing?" Clearly, there's a time and place for us to ask those sorts of questions. Without tending to these issues, we have no community and the church can't grow into the kind of people God wants us to be.

However, God's plan has a side B—as outlined in the Great Commission texts. In our quest for personal healing and wholeness, we can't forget about the world that God so loved that he sent his Son, Jesus, to die for it. God also has in mind to build "outwardly focused" groups. Side B is what this book is about. We are putting into action an approach to encountering our city—one person at a time. With each act of love and generosity, we can make a difference.

SOME PROJECT GUIDELINES

What If Things Go Wrong When We Are Doing Our Outreach?

Being a veteran of outreach projects, I believe that question is best answered by quoting Tarzan: "What mean 'if'?" In other words, a few things will definitely go haywire when groups begin to do servant evangelism. While the projects outlined in this book are, for the most part, pretty simple, something can go wrong. My church has been doing outreach projects for many years. We highly value planning, yet almost every time we go out, a little something goes a little wrong. Here's the lesson to learn: It's best to have a flexible, teachable attitude as you reach out. And don't forget to practice smiling as you do it!

Where Should We Go?

Your choice of location will be determined by the flow and type of people you're trying to reach. In most cases I like to touch as many people as possible, so I usually choose high-traffic areas. It's feasible to go door to door in your neighborhood to offer a serving project; just be careful not to come back too often or the residents will begin to feel harassed.

Go to where the people are who you feel led by God to reach. That's campuses for college students; that's bike trails for recreational types. But keep in mind there are some subtler areas of town that need to be discovered by your group. For example, certain apartments are filled with single-parent families. Or your group may feel led to get involved in a mercy ministry to the poor. A great place to find needy people is in the government-subsidized housing areas in your city as well as in certain parts where the elderly are living on fixed incomes. The key is to go out and take notes as you do. Return to the most fruitful places. I've found that those locations where people don't respond well during the first outreach or two tend not to get better in the long run. Don't waste your time on a bad location.

What About Kids? Can We Bring Them Along?

Kids can make a great addition to the serving team, provided the projects match their maturity and skills. For example, children can do aspects of a car wash (like washing wheels). Some projects described here definitely don't work well with children, but a patient parent with a little creativity can involve a child in just about anything. My hope as a parent is always to give my children a positive experience with servant evangelism, so I always make it part of the routine to take them to McDonald's afterward and treat them to a Happy Meal.

How Often Should We Go Out?

The frequency for outings needs to be worked out with your group. Your group may be filled with extroverts who are dying to get out on the streets. On the other hand, maybe you have a fairly introverted bunch that would rather conduct a Bible study. Both need to get out with some regularity for the sake of the group's health. With outreach, it's always a matter of how much, how often.

I suggest that a group go out to do a project at every fourth meeting. Some of our groups meet weekly, while others meet every other week. In the first case, the groups would go out every month; in the second case, the groups would go out every other month.

Before coming to a hard-and-fast decision about how often you will do outreach, venture out a few times with these projects. Be experimental. See what works and what doesn't and how your group responds to the flow of the outreach. If your group finds tremendous affinity with these projects, consider doing them more often.

How Long Should We Go Out?

While it can be a lot of fun to do servant evangelism projects, you need to monitor just how long you work at them. It becomes difficult to maintain the energy of the group if you make outreach too long. In our history of doing these projects, groups at my church have found that most people can't sustain a high level of enthusiasm on a project for more than about two hours. While the first time or two out doing these projects may well be exciting (and even thrilling if you have been stuck with an inward focus as a group), don't make the mistake of taxing your group with more ministry than it can sustain. Two hours is plenty of time for doing an outreach—including gathering, giving instructions, traveling to the outreach site, doing the outreach for a little over an hour, and reconvening to share stories.

What's the Most Important Practical Point to Keep in Mind?

Be organized. If you make your people wait because you're not prepared, you'll waste their time and diminish their zeal for future outreaches. If you're the leader, do your behind-the-scenes preparation plenty in advance so that when your people arrive, everything is ready to go. Make sure you have permission (if necessary) to be where you're doing the outreach. Provide twice as much material as you think you'll need. Your people's time is your most valuable asset. Let them know that you value them by being ready for them long before they arrive to reach out with Christ's love.

What's the Best Way to Make Your People Feel Successful?

Tell success stories. Keep track of the good encounters that take place with your serving outings. It's easy to get caught up in the practical matters of planning and executing a project and then, once it's over, to busy yourself with putting away equipment and so on. Don't forget to reflect! Your people need to have a time of storytelling to solidify what just happened in their hearts. These stories will become a part of the larger history of your group. In the months and years to come, your people will reflect back and say, "Remember the time we did that for those people? That was a great time. We really did something significant when . . ." Your people won't forget these events in the years to come. Every group needs a history. Outreach is a strong history-making activity.

What Do We Say When Interacting with Those We Serve?

When asked, "So why are you doing this?" teams from my church often say, "We're here today doing a community service project to show you God's love in a practical way." That simple statement has enough content to spark further conversation about the love of Christ. It has worked for us thousands of times. I recommend you memorize it and use it as a standard response line when serving.

Sometimes I say to people, "If Jesus were in town today, walking about, I think he'd be both saying things and doing things. This is the sort of thing he'd be doing for people." That usually makes sense to totally unchurched people.

At other times I say, "We're here today living out what the Bible says. Instead of handing people something and saying, 'Here, read this,' we're here saying, 'Here, experience this.'" (For more ideas, see "What to Say" on pages 106-107.)

What About Verbalizing the Gospel with Them?

Be ready to respond to people based on wherever they are spiritually. The key is to pay attention to their signals. In my experience, I've found it's a mistake to attempt to share the same exact thing with every single person we serve. When it comes to verbalizing the gospel, your teams may fall prey to two different dangers: saying too much too soon (sE—a small amount of "s," serving; a large amount of "E," evangelism); or serving too much and forgetting to evangelize (Se—a large amount of serving, "S," while minimizing the message of the gospel, "e," by missing opportunities to verbalize the good news).

Sometimes, by being overly aggressive, we inadvertently communicate to people a message of conditional love, that is, "God loves you only if you agree with us." What's the balance? I think we need to be trained in both traditional evangelism approaches as well as the servant evangelism approaches outlined in this book.

When I'm out doing servant evangelism, I bring along gospel

tracts to share with those who are "ripe" and responsive—certainly there are many of those we encounter along the way. I liken the process of evangelism to the game of golf. In golf there are long shots made with wood clubs. There are medium shots made with iron clubs. But those shots that are up close to the hole are made with a putter. People tend to be at different distances from the hole, or to the point of declaring faith in Christ. Some we meet will be in greatest need of a wood shot to bring them toward Christ from quite a distance. I think those people will be most vulnerable to the power of kindness. Those who have found their way partially forward have questions about the faith; they need the iron shot of an apologetics conversation. That is, they need some conversations before they can make further progress forward. Finally, those near the hole only need someone to help pray with them—to apply the putter and sink the ball in the hole.

As you go into the community, steadily encountering people at different levels of receptivity, you need to be sensitive to where they are in their progress. If you're going to be effective in outreach, your goal must be to serve. Memorizing a pat response to use with everyone you encounter will not work. Share your faith in a spirit of servanthood.

Throughout this book you will see references to "connection cards." These cards, which are given to those you serve, explain what has been done to them. The act of servant evangelism outreach projects is a rather hit-or-miss affair. That is, sometimes you will have complete conversations with those being served, and other times you will simply not have the opportunity to converse adequately. It is important that those being touched with these acts of kindness have some means of getting back in touch with you if they so desire.

Here is an example of a connection card my church uses. Feel free to use it exactly as it is printed, or play with the wording and graphics as you see fit. (Our card wording and graphics are also available as downloadable files at our website, *www.servantevangelism.com*.) In essence, you need to briefly explain what you are doing, then offer a phone number, address, website, and so on for follow-up.

Are There Any Secrets to Making This Work?

Do as good a job as possible. Let's leave everyone we touch with a positive impression of both the love and the quality of Christ.

Smile while you serve! A cheery face is incredibly disarming, not to mention that it keeps everyone up emotionally.

Don't be distressed when you're denied the opportunity to serve. I've found that the real power in our serving projects is in the *offer* to serve, even more than in the *action* of serving. Inevitably, you will be denied when you offer to serve others. Not to worry! Those you touch with the offer will leave emotionally and spiritually curious about your generosity.

Learn to tell your own story about how you came to know Christ. You need to have a few versions of your testimony: a short one that can be conveyed in a minute, a longer one of three minutes, and a more extensive one that can be given over a cup of coffee. Most of the conversations you'll have with people connected with servant evangelism projects will only allow for one- to three-minute interactions. No matter what the specifics are of your story, it's powerful. Look for opportunities to share it. When someone asks an open-ended question like "So, what motivates someone to come out on a day like this to clean toilets?" (I've gotten that question dozens of times!) That's someone who is saying, "Please give me your testimony."

In short, your testimony should include these basic elements:

1. I used to not have a relationship with Christ.
2. Something happened and I began to believe.
3. That faith in Jesus has made all the difference in the world to me.

Will This Be Any Fun?

Sometimes in the course of pulling off an outreach we can forget the obvious—to enjoy ourselves. I live by the adage, "Where the Spirit of the Lord is, there is fun!" (a near-quote of 2 Corinthians 3:17). I've found that to be true throughout my Christian life.

The inverse is true as well: where there is true, good, clean fun, usually the Spirit of the Lord is found as well. I think that one of the most compelling reasons for doing servant evangelism projects is the fun factor. This stuff of going into the community to serve our way into hearts just makes for an incredibly good time.

If you aren't enjoying yourselves as you reach out with the kindness of God, you'll come across oddly to those you serve. It's out of place to say with your mouths, "Hi, this is to show you the love of God," but to show a lemon-sour frown on your faces.

How Should We Debrief as a Group?
After an outreach, it's a good idea to have a time set aside to do some downloading. Gather back where you started and share over a cup of coffee or a hamburger what happened. The stories will mostly be very positive. Occasionally, someone will have a bit of a challenging outing. But this storytelling time is a great opportunity to encourage everyone onward in his or her experience. The ones who had a slam-dunk positive experience have a need to share that story with others so that they might be encouraged. The positive stories will also allow the timid people to reinterpret their experience in the safety of the larger group.

You might even bring along a video camera to capture some of your outreach experiences permanently. Many of the projects outlined in this book come across very well on video and make for encouraging, fun viewing later. We often tape an outreach and then show it immediately afterward, during a brief downloading time, as a way to consolidate the time with the participants. It may be corny, but people love to see themselves on video.

How Do We Pay for These Projects?
I abide by a particular principle when it comes to starting out with outreach: If you wait until you have all the financial questions answered before you go into action, you will never go into action.

For this reason I've adopted the operational credo, "Ready, Fire! Aim." When we take a Ready, Fire, Aim approach to ministry, we're more apt to move by the power of faith rather than sight. From the beginning of our outreach orientation we have followed the adage, "Money follows momentum." You may be a small group of just a few individuals. Pray, then look for what God provides, but know for certain that he will provide. He is certainly interested in reaching your city. He'll make provision.

As you progress in your outreaches, I recommend you make the commitment to reach your city a priority within your church's budget. My church has given at least 15 percent of our income to local evangelism since the beginning of our church's launch. That number would be difficult to jump into for most existing churches. A more realistic, yet significant enough amount to start with is perhaps 5 percent. I'm confident that as you faithfully do these projects you'll generate enough positive fruit that the money spent will be an obviously good investment.

Pray

The servant evangelism approach to outreach is action-oriented, but as we reach out we dare not underestimate the importance of prayer. As you step out to serve, you'll be naturally inclined to pray for God's blessing as you serve. Only those who have stood on a traffic island with a box of donuts while waiting for the traffic light to change can relate to the truth of the statement "We need God's blessing for this to work." As you serve, do it with a spirit of humility and dependence on the Holy Spirit's power for success. Without his blessing on us, we simply are pleasant people doing nice things for others.

I always react when people call what we do "random acts of kindness." There is nothing random about what we are doing. We move in "empowered kindness," and we change people's lives as we touch them in significant ways by the power of the Holy Spirit. Romans 2:4 couldn't be more clear on this point: *"the kindness of God leads you to repentance"* (NASB).

I make a habit of gathering the team to pray briefly before going out on an outreach project. I encourage team members to pray all the while they are serving—to pray for success, to pray for those they are serving, to pray for open doors of opportunity, to pray for the right people to come along as they serve. And then, upon returning from serving, we pray for those we touched—that Christ will have his way in each of their lives and that they will come into the family of God.

Keep on Praying

The concepts of "prayer walking" and servant evangelism go hand in hand. (In fact, I recommend the book *Prayer-Walking* by Steve Hawthorne and Graham Kendrick, Creation House, 1993.) My church has often seen areas where we would like to do outreaches closed to us for one reason or another—liability concerns, safety issues, or the age-old "Gee, we've never done that before" response. Many times, after we have done on-site prayer (low key, as modeled in the prayer-walking concept) we've seen the doors of ministry open amazingly wide to us.

We tried for twelve years to get our foot in the door to do Christmas gift-wrapping at one of the largest, nicest malls in our city. Each of our attempts was met with a cordial but firm no. Finally, we began to prayer walk that mall each week. Within six months, out of the blue, they called us and asked if we would like to do a gift-wrapping outreach! In this one mall alone, we can serve more than one hundred thousand people each holiday season. That's quite an answer to persistent prayer.

Go Out

The projects outlined in this book are not complicated. I call them the "classic Volkswagen Beetle of evangelism"—that is, it's pretty simple, and there aren't that many moving parts.

Begin to experiment with these concepts by putting them into practice. Honestly, there isn't a lot that can go wrong with the projects outlined in these pages. The rejection you might face is minimal. When we go out to give away soft drinks, for example, about the worst we hear is someone getting mad because they want a Pepsi when we're giving away Cokes. You can handle that level of rejection!

Get a couple of friends, pick a level 1 project that looks interesting, and just get started.

Keep Going Out

If you hope to make an impression on your neighborhoods, you need to consistently connect and then reconnect through serving projects. In other words, make a commitment to your community for a set period, and follow through on that commitment before analyzing the apparent results. I recommend you mentally sign up for six month's worth of outreaches to begin with. During this time you'll experience at least a couple changes of seasons and hopefully a dozen or so of the projects listed in this book that fit your situation.

As I mentioned, you will have a mixture of mostly positive and a few negative experiences as you reach out. Don't let the highs get you overly excited and don't take the negatives too close to heart. I've found that if a group commits to going out to do outreach monthly for six months, they'll see enough encouraging fruit from their efforts to keep doing outreach over a longer term.

Leaders Take the Lead

Before you go out as a group, I recommend that the leader(s) of your group go out first to get the ball rolling. Look over the list of beginning projects at the end of this book (pages 108-110) for some starter projects to ponder. The idea here is to experience it first before leading the others into it. Like it or not, people do what their leaders do, not what they say. Begin to do what you want the people you lead to emulate. They'll follow your lead.

"Come and See" or "Go and Do"?

As you read Scripture, you can find two equally biblical slogans: "Come and see" and "Go and do." Many churches like to quote what Philip said to skeptical Nathanael: "Come and see" (John 1:46). That phrase has been so popular that it is posted on the welcome signs of many churches. It's not a bad slogan. "Come and see" what the Lord is doing in our midst. "Come and see" the love of Christ that's present here.

I remember the first time I saw those words on the side of a church. I was in high school. I was not a Christian yet, and the idea intrigued me. I wondered, "What's going on in that place?" For whatever level of effectiveness that phrase may have had at one point, I believe it is a mistake to use it as a guiding philosophy these days.

Author and statistician George Barna writes that those who don't attend church are no longer so much unchurched as they are dechurched. They have, at least in their minds, checked out the church. They've evaluated it and found it irrelevant to their lives and needs. "Come and see" is not going to connect with people of our age.

Also, I believe that phrase subtly builds a mindset that is dangerous to our people. It implies that something wonderful is going on here that is just so great that if the people of our city could just see it we're sure they would want to join us. I suspect — as a leader in the body of Christ, I hope — that there is something wonderful going on with most churches and most small groups. Sure, if our cities could experience the wonder and beauty of the fellowship we experience, they would very possibly want to join us.

But, to quote Joan Rivers, "Can we talk?" Most people aren't going to just stumble across our door. They aren't going to, by happenstance, "come and see." If there is any hope of our city coming to know Jesus, we must adopt in a wholesale way the motto "Go and do." Our only problem is, "How in the world can we do that?"

Play Safe

Two smartly dressed businessmen sat across the restaurant table with forlorn looks on their faces. Judging by their earlier phone call to me, I felt they were like most small group leaders I know — frustrated with outreach. They knew that reaching out beyond themselves was vital for the health of their groups, but they didn't have a clue as to how to do that in a healthy way. However, these two were at least stepping out to try to do something with outreach. Their long faces were begging the question, so I had to ask, "What happens when your groups try to do evangelism?"

"It's weird—every time we schedule an outreach event, none of our members show up."

"Well, what sort of outreach events are you attempting?"

"Every month, on the first Saturday, we drive around looking for hitchhikers. When we find one, we give them a ride, buy them lunch, and share the gospel with them. Then at Christmas we do an outreach to the homeless who live down by the river. We buy them food and blankets, then we pray for them."

Sitting in the restaurant I had to admire their sheer guts. They were certainly getting out of their box! They had great hearts and even the right idea. Outreach is vital to the health of every small group. Their problem: they were going about it in a scary way. Let's face it, not many average suburban small-group members will jump at the chance to go into a crack neighborhood at Christmas!

The enthusiasm level of their groups was beginning to dwindle because the groups were only inwardly focused. Like most small groups, they were naturals at nurture, but lacked an outward, practical reason for their existence. In my twenty years of leading and coaching small groups, I've come to conclude that one constant is present in all groups that remain healthy, reproduce, and stay viable for the long haul: they regularly reach out beyond themselves.

How Can We Reach Out?
My business friends had the right idea in going to the homeless; it's just that they were biting off more than they could handle. A catch phrase I hear a lot these days is that we need to set "big, hairy, audacious goals." Well, big goals are fine, but there is such a thing as *goal overload.* Going to the homeless was a good idea, but it was too much.

I encouraged these leaders to be strategic. That is, I suggested that they start doing outreach in small ways that will give people in their groups successful experiences at first. Once those group members have had several small positive experiences with outreach, then the elements of depth, risk, and complication can be added as the groups grow in faithfulness and confidence.

Three Levels of Outreach Involvement
Well, this book isn't really about small groups. It's about one aspect of small-group life—reaching out in servant evangelism as an important way of keeping the overall condition of the group in good health.

So let's talk about servant evangelism and outreach. The progression of outreach looks like this:

Blitzing > Connecting > Investing

All three of these approaches and their levels of outreach have their place. However, to build success you need to be aware of your group's skill, confidence level, and resources. My recommendation is that, as you read and apply this book, you start with the blitzing level projects to gain momentum. If your group is like most I've met, you probably have little forward progress going right now with evangelism. Get the ball rolling in the right direction with a few of the level 1 (blitzing) projects. Then progress to the level 2 (connecting) projects. As you feel adventurous, go on to the level 3 (investing) outreaches.

LEVEL 1
THE BLITZ

EVERYBODY NEEDS A PLACE to start—for small-group outreaches it's the Blitz. These adrenaline-pumping projects are designed to touch a lot of people in a short time. They're a great way to involve team members in reaching out together to touch the community in simple yet meaningful ways. This level of outreach usually involves some products, so there is a financial cost involved, but nothing that your group can't afford.

Blitzing projects are great for the following:

- getting your people involved with an *action* orientation
- doing something that doesn't take a long *time* to pull off
- creating quick *momentum* (In about six months, your church or small group can become quite well known for its blitzing visibility in the city. Many will think you are larger in number than you actually are because of your many outreaches.)
- building initial evangelism *confidence* (You can always try more risky projects later if you feel led.)
- expanding *vision* (All of these projects are a great place to get more ideas for outreach.)
- seeing the *potential* for reaching out to the entire city with outreach projects such as these

1 SOFT DRINK GIVEAWAY
(5+ PER TEAM)

ON A HOT AFTERNOON, there's nothing like a cold drink to soothe people's thirst. A Diet Coke may not be exactly what Jesus had in mind when he spoke of giving away a cup of cold water (Matthew 10:42), but at least it's cold!

Do this in an area with a lot of traffic, either on foot or by car. Set up on a busy corner with a stop light. When the light turns red, with a couple of drinks in hand your team can ask motorists, "Would you like a diet or regular?" That simple introduction often becomes additional conversation regarding why you are doing this project. Answer by saying, "Jesus met practical and spiritual needs. It's hot today, so we are here doing what he would do in a modern package."

If the idea of locating at an intersection sounds too risky, try the entrance of a grocery store during a high-traffic hour. You will need to contact the manager in advance to explain your project. Customers are more chatty and easygoing on their way into the grocery store, and are typically in a rush to get to their cars on the way out. Therefore, you will have more success setting up at the entrance of the store.

You will need several signs that read, "Totally Free Drinks!" Ice the drinks down an hour or so before the outreach so they're refreshing when given away. You'll need a prep table to set the drinks on once you've taken them out of the coolers. In case you don't get adequate time to explain your project to shoppers, place a card explaining the project under each can's tab.

WHERE TO GO

- Campuses
- Parks
- Neighborhoods
- Sporting Events
- Downtown
- Commuters
- Shopping Centers

WHAT YOU'LL NEED

- ☐ Soft drinks in cans
- ☐ Ice
- ☐ Coolers
- ☐ Three to four signs: "Totally Free Drinks!"
- ☐ Folding table
- ☐ Towel (for drying the drinks off before attaching the connection cards)
- ☐ Connection cards

(Ours say, "You looked too thirsty to pass up! We hope this drink brought some relief to your day. If we can be of more help, please give us a call.")

The drink giveaway is one of the most expensive projects you can do, but it's great for getting started and having a high-energy experience. If you buy the drinks in quantities, you can probably negotiate a discount. Our small groups typically give away about two hundred drinks at a single outreach. You'll need to experiment with the brand of drinks you offer and the percentage of diets to regulars. Some parts of town might even prefer bottled water or juices to carbonated drinks.

When approaching those you are serving, don't ask, "Would you like a free drink?" That phrase gives people a chance to quickly brush you off. A much better, more positive way to talk to people is to smile, with a diet in one hand and a regular in the other, and to ask, "Would you like a diet or a regular? It's free!" Be irresistible as you approach people.

IN ACTION: On Election Day in South Africa, a church in Johannesburg did a gigantic soft drink outreach to voters as they stood in line to cast their votes. The voting lines were enormous—voters waited for up to three hours to use their newfound privilege. This simple act of generosity was greatly appreciated by these voters. The color barriers came down quickly, and some great conversations took place between blacks, whites, and Asians—all because someone offered a stranger a free soft drink.

2 GASOLINE BUY-DOWN
(10+ PER TEAM)

HOW WOULD YOU LIKE to do an outreach that will get so much attention you might even create a traffic jam? When you lower the price of gasoline for a couple of hours, you'll attract no small attention to your act of generosity. You might even make the evening news!

This project needs to be set up a week or two in advance by connecting with the station manager first. The essence of the project is this: Lower the price of gasoline for a set time (usually an hour or two). If it's normally $1.50 per gallon, lower it to $1.25 for that time and pay the difference to the station at the end of the time. The key is to lower the price to the point that it will get the attention of passing motorists.

Provide services to the customers during that time. Offer to wash their windshields while their gasoline tank is filling. If time allows, check the oil levels.

Provide signs during the set time

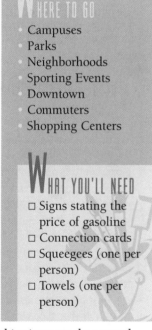

WHERE TO GO
- Campuses
- Parks
- Neighborhoods
- Sporting Events
- Downtown
- Commuters
- Shopping Centers

WHAT YOU'LL NEED
- ☐ Signs stating the price of gasoline
- ☐ Connection cards
- ☐ Squeegees (one per person)
- ☐ Towels (one per person)

with the "new and improved" prices. Put a big sign over the normal price sign, but also have some people holding hand signs that read, "$1.25 Gasoline!" to get people's attention.

While doing the serving, explain what you are doing and why you are doing it, and give out connection cards explaining the project.

Big national chain stations are usually bound by organizational policy and are not able to participate in projects like this. These stations tend to be fearful of liability issues. However, locally owned ones are usually very open to the idea. If you're turned down at the first place or two, persevere; the idea is worth hanging in there with.

You might wonder, "But doesn't that cost a lot?" It costs less than you might think. The total usually adds up to two or three hundred dollars for a two-hour project. Considering the dollar amount and the manpower needed, this is an outreach that's best taken on by more than one group at a time.

When the generosity of God is demonstrated, people take notice.

 IN ACTION: The first time we did the gasoline buy-down we made it onto a big AM radio station's traffic report. The helicopter DJ came on and said, "I don't know what's happening down on the corner there, but there's a significant traffic jam. Someone just called in to the station and said something about gasoline twenty-five cents off the regular price. Something about showing God's love in a practical way. If I were you, I'd get in my car and get over there."

DONUT GIVEAWAY DURING MORNING TRAFFIC
(5+ PER TEAM)

WHO CAN RESIST A pastry at the stop light on the way to work? Buy a few hundred glazed and chocolate donuts (get the quantity discount; glazed donuts are about the easiest for motorists to handle while driving). Set up at a freeway off ramp, on a traffic island, or at a long traffic light—anywhere that affords enough time to step into traffic with your box of pastries. Don't handle the donuts with your hands.

As with the soft drink giveaway, don't ask, "Would you like a donut?" Rather the question is "Which would you prefer, a glazed or a chocolate?" They get a donut, a connection card, a very brief explanation of what's going on, and something to ponder on their way to work.

If you find evening outreaches difficult for your group, this one fits the bill. If your typical 8 to 5 business people can go to work just a little late, they will be able to pull this one off with no trouble and touch a hundred or so people—all before the beginning of the workday.

This is a very quick, high-volume ministry that is full of little ten-second conversations. You'll have to be brief with your comments—you're in traffic, after all. A word of caution: In your enthusiasm, watch the traffic signals. Designate someone on your team as a traffic person to keep an eye on the changing traffic lights.

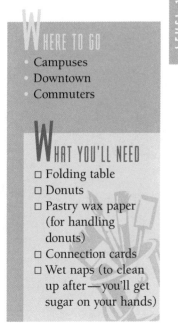

IN ACTION: Donuts are not as popular in Kenya as they are in the United States, but people still eat breakfast. A group of creative Christians there came up with the idea of giving away bananas during morning drive times. They attach a connection card to the banana with a rubber band. The outreach is so popular, they are becoming known in their city as the "banana Christians"—a name that doesn't sound so nice in English, but fits the Kenyan culture just fine.

WHERE TO GO

- Campuses
- Downtown
- Commuters

WHAT YOU'LL NEED

- ☐ Folding table
- ☐ Donuts
- ☐ Pastry wax paper (for handling donuts)
- ☐ Connection cards
- ☐ Wet naps (to clean up after—you'll get sugar on your hands)

4 ASSORTED GIVEAWAYS
(5+ PER TEAM)

EVERYONE LIKES TO GET something for free, especially if it can be eaten. Our church has given away different kinds of treats over the years, and they all seem to work well. The key to doing a giveaway is to locate somewhere with a high traffic flow. In Cincinnati, we frequent Reds baseball games where we make several thousand "touches" with incoming fans in the hour before the game.

One summer we gave away literally hundreds of thousands of pieces of taffy—something that is popular and very affordable. To bring the price down we approached an area candy manufacturer and explained our outreach concept. He gave us a great deal.

Chewing gum (by the pack) can be purchased in large quantities for a reasonable price. Large versions of a single piece of candy (for example, one-inch diameter LifeSaver candies in the single pack) can be purchased at Sam's Club stores nationwide. Attach an appropriate connection card, and you're on your way.

It's difficult to determine how many items you'll need when you first begin with giveaway projects. It will take a few trial runs to determine the particular likes and dislikes of the people you're serving. LifeSavers may go over in a big way, while chewing gum may be a bust. You just have to experiment. I recommend you be prepared with a lot of materials each time you go out to do ministry. That is, if you're buying LifeSavers, buy far more than you think you'll possibly need. With any outreach, there is both an emotional cost and a material goods cost. The material end of the equation is always the least expensive factor you'll deal with. It's always better to have some left over than to have people who want to do more ministry but run out of materials.

Purchase what you give away versus giving away homemade goods. While your homemade chocolate chip cookies are probably of better quality than the individually packaged ones, there will be a resistance from most people to receiving unsealed goods. Like it or not, it's a sign of the times we live in.

Some items that are perhaps rather costly when purchased at a retail store can be bought in bulk at a significant discount. The place to start with bulk purchasing is discount warehouses like Costco, Sam's Club, Wal-Mart, or Target.

After you get your feet wet in the giveaway ministry, consider diversifying with more-exotic items. For example, we've been giving out chemical hand warmers—something football fans enthusiastically receive at fall and winter sporting events. (The warmers stay hot for two hours when the packing seal is broken—a nifty invention.) These cost about $1.50 retail at hardware stores, but when purchased by the case they are only twenty-one cents—affordable for any group!

WHERE TO GO

- Campuses
- Parks
- Neighborhoods
- Sporting Events
- Downtown
- Commuters
- Shopping Centers

WHAT YOU'LL NEED

- ☐ Connection cards
- ☐ Giveaway product (LifeSavers, taffy, chewing gum, cookies, peanuts, pencils, pens, sunglasses, or other small items)
- ☐ Canvas bags to carry the product
- ☐ Rubber bands to attach the connection cards

5 DOLLAR DROP OR QUARTER DROP
(3+ PER TEAM)

DO YOU HAVE A place in mind in town to reach out to, but it's off limits? One project we've had a great response to is the Dollar Drop. Malls are usually difficult places to get permission to go about any sort of outreach. For years I tried in vain to get into some of the largest malls in Cincinnati to do servant evangelism. The downtown areas of most cities, which business people frequent at lunch, also are prime locations to do outreaches, but ones that are typically difficult to break into, even with the approachable means of servant evangelism. So how about giving away money? No kidding. If they thought pennies were from heaven, just wait until they find a dollar! With a little bit of rubber cement, attach a connection card to a dollar.

I usually take a stack of them and drop them one at a time in various places around the mall. You can do this anywhere, but I prefer the mall, where people travel in groups. It won't take long before someone notices the dollar. One of the senses built into humans is the ability to sense the presence of money lying on the ground. When they find the dollar, they pick it up, read the card, and usually pass it back and forth to one another.

A less expensive version of this is the Quarter Drop. Have you ever noticed people who habitually check vending machines and pay-phone coin returns for change? Print a connection sticker that's slightly larger than a quarter and place it on the back side. Put these in coin returns of various sorts as well as in the penny trays at convenience stores. The stickers come off easily when the customers want to use the quarters.

It is great fun to watch people find the money that you leave lying around. The responses are priceless. Some actually shout out loud, "A dollar bill!" It's a real attention-getter.

WHERE TO GO

- Campuses
- Parks
- Neighborhoods
- Sporting Events
- Downtown
- Shopping Centers

WHAT YOU'LL NEED

- ☐ Dollar bills/quarters
- ☐ Connection cards/connection stickers
- ☐ Removable adhesive

 **IN ACTION:** In fiscally conservative Holland we discovered that people were stunned at the sight of a guilder lying on the sidewalk. When pedestrians stopped to pick up the coin, along with the connection card that explained our project ("This guilder is a free gift to you—because God loves you!"), they had a variety of responses. Surprisingly, many stunned pedestrians stopped, read the note, kept the connection card, and left the guilder on the ground! We have tried this project in a number of cultures and have found, not surprisingly, that people everywhere notice money lying on the sidewalk.

6 DOLLAR TIPPING OF RESTAURANT SERVERS
(3+ PER TEAM)

I WORKED MY WAY through college as a waiter at a number of different restaurants. I found that tips typically ranged from 10 to 20 percent. Unfortunately, true or not, church people had the reputation of being lousy tippers. By growing in our tipping generosity, we can go a long way toward changing the perception that Christians are stingy.

WHERE TO GO

- Campuses
- Neighborhoods
- Downtown
- Shopping Centers

WHAT YOU'LL NEED

- ☐ Dollar bills
- ☐ Connection cards

This is a simple but profound outreach that will get restaurants buzzing with excitement. Bring a number of one-dollar bills (I usually make it ten to twenty dollars). While sitting at my table talking with friends, I hand each waitress who passes by a dollar with a connection card. I say, "I'll bet you haven't been tipped enough lately. Here's a little to make a small difference."

I usually get responses like "There must be some mistake. I'm not your waitress," or "You really don't have to do this," or "I don't know what to say. No one has ever tipped me for no reason before." All of these responses are comments that open the door for short but fruitful conversations. Often, after I've handed out a number of tips, the word of my outreach spreads to the manager and he makes his way to my table to ask why I'm doing this. It's great fun.

 IN ACTION: On one of the first tipping outreach experiments we conducted as a staff (see pages 36-37 for more details on how that works), one of our pastors informed me he was simply too busy to participate in this outreach. I told him I thought that surely there must be something he could do to invest his twenty dollars to show some people the love of Christ. In a moment of quick brainstorming, I asked, "Aren't you going out to eat at a restaurant right now? Do the tipping outreach. Give a dollar to every waiter you see—whether they help you or not. Let me know what happens."

When I saw him later that afternoon, he was clearly moved from his noontime outreach: "Each waiter I tipped was amazed. They all said, 'No one has ever tipped me when I didn't deserve it before.' But the best one of the day was the woman who came up to the table with a bit of a dazed look on her face. She said, 'Today is my first day on the job. Your tip is my first dollar—and you said it was from God. Can you give me directions to your church? I want to check out a place that gives tips to people.'" I'm not sure who was more touched, the restaurant staff who got the dollars or my friend who realized that significant outreach can take place during a lunch break.

7 TRASH PICK-UP WITH "KINDNESS IN PROGRESS" SIGNS
(3+ PER TEAM)

HERE'S A PROJECT THAT will test the "servant of all" concept in your group. While doing this one I've been asked many times, "So, did you get arrested for driving while intoxicated or something? Did the police put you to work on the side of the road?"

People in passing cars toss litter in front of retail stores, gasoline stations, and restaurants. While store managers tend to pick up debris in their immediate parking lot, the area by the street often gets overlooked. Also, the off ramp from a highway to a street is usually a spot filled with bottles, cigarettes, fast food litter, and more. Show up in teams and pick up trash to show God's love in a practical way to motorists and merchants.

Make this project something that plays on the curiosity of the passersby. Beginning the day before (usually a Friday), put up "Kindness in Progress" signs (several of them; they should be about the size of real estate signs) on the side of the road where you will be cleaning. The next day (usually a Saturday), show up wearing vests with "Kindness in Progress" on the back. Be equipped with gloves, trash pick-up sticks, and plastic bags for the trash you will gather.

Before you begin, approach the managers of the nearby businesses

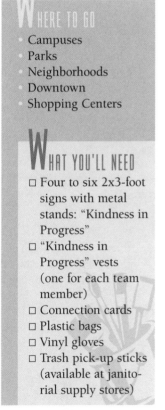

WHERE TO GO
- Campuses
- Parks
- Neighborhoods
- Downtown
- Shopping Centers

WHAT YOU'LL NEED
- ☐ Four to six 2x3-foot signs with metal stands: "Kindness in Progress"
- ☐ "Kindness in Progress" vests (one for each team member)
- ☐ Connection cards
- ☐ Plastic bags
- ☐ Vinyl gloves
- ☐ Trash pick-up sticks (available at janitorial supply stores)

to explain the projects. Say, "We are doing a community service project today out on ____ Street by picking up debris. We're showing God's love to the merchants today in a practical way. Here's our card [give a connection card]. We hope we've been an encouragement to you today. If we can be of more help, give us a call." Leave the signs up until Sunday or Monday evening so that the drive-time people can see the difference you've made since Friday afternoon.

Some outreach team members wonder what good it is to pick up trash. In Cincinnati as we go out regularly to certain locations, drivers know what we are doing now, and they honk and wave in affirmation as they drive by. As we pick up debris with signs explaining what we're doing, thousands of people drive by and see the church in action. If this becomes a regular thing, the people of your community will begin to associate the church with service. Not a bad image!

IN ACTION: In Eldoret, Kenya, a church gathered several dozen small groups together at once to pick up litter in their city. Their unusual act of kindness caught the eye of a newspaper reporter. The result: the next day a very positive front-page article and photo in the national newspaper covered their outreach. The reporter asked, "So why are you picking up trash in your city streets?" One Christian replied, "We think that if Jesus Christ were in Kenya today he would, among other things, be serving people by picking up trash. So we're picking up trash."

8 TWENTY-DOLLAR OUTREACH EXPERIMENT
(5+ PARTICIPANTS)

IF YOU'RE STARTING FROM scratch with servant evangelism, you might consider launching in an exciting way by participating in the Twenty-Dollar Outreach Experiment. The rules are simple: Everyone in your group agrees to do some sort of outreach during the next week. They'll each invest twenty dollars on this project. Throw out a few ideas as covered in this book to get the ball rolling, but challenge the group to be creative with their investment. As a result of this experiment, you'll learn a lot about what works and what doesn't in your part of town.

To make your feat a little bit more fun, award a few prizes for various categories of creativity—for example, "The Most Daring Project," "The Most Creative Project," "The Most People Touched Award." Celebrate the creativity that God has given to your group.

Record for posterity the various efforts made among your individuals or groups. It's likely that one or more of these projects will work later as a group project or on an even larger scale. Share your outreach adventures with other small groups to encourage them. Even if you don't do that particular project again, they may. (If you come up with new ideas, I'd love to hear about them. E-mail me via our website, www.servantevangelism.com.)

The Twenty-Dollar Outreach Experiment is something that can also work later in your group's life to reinvigorate an outward focus after it has gotten the idea of servant evangelism under its belt. That is, when you want to shake things up a bit, do another experiment. Your only instruction to the group is "You can do anything with the money as long as it's not illegal, immoral, or unsafe. Now come back next week with some exciting stories!" Some of our best projects have come out of these weeklong experiments.

WHERE TO GO

- Campuses
- Parks
- Neighborhoods
- Sporting Events
- Downtown
- Commuters
- Shopping Centers

WHAT YOU'LL NEED

- ☐ Twenty-dollar bill
- ☐ Prizes!
- ☐ Response sheet
- ☐ Connection cards

9 NEWSPAPER GIVEAWAY
(5+ PARTICIPANTS)

PEOPLE FROM ALL WALKS of life read the newspaper. Every once in a while, surprise them with a freebie. This project will work in any city, in any culture, on any day of the week—and in any weather condition!

Buy newspapers directly from the publisher in bulk quantities. Give these out at stop lights in a way similar to the soft drink giveaway. When the light turns red, step out into traffic briefly and offer motorists a newspaper with a connection card attached.

Instead of using the connection card, you can design a sticker (similar to the one for the Quarter Drop, pages 32-33) and apply these to the front of the paper.

A variation of this project is to go into a convenience store and approach the manager with this offer: "We'd like to purchase your entire stack of newspapers to give them to your customers for free. Could you just put this sign ["Newspapers free today courtesy of _____ Church"] on top of the stack?" The manager will inevitably have a

WHERE TO GO

- Campuses
- Parks
- Neighborhoods
- Sporting Events
- Downtown
- Commuters
- Shopping Centers

WHAT YOU'LL NEED

□ Newspapers
□ Rubber bands
□ Connection stickers
□ "Kindness in
   Progress" vests (ideal,
   but not necessary)

number of questions, and you can share about how the love of Christ is motivating you to do this project. In the end, you'll usually get permission to do it. Leave connection cards with the manager to give out with the newspapers.

IN ACTION: This may sound rather odd—a sort of self-service outreach—but it has worked well for us in Cincinnati. The store employees end up explaining the project in their own words, which gets them curious about the gospel ("I wonder why these people would give these papers away."). The question raised on this project is whether there's any value in one nonChristian talking to another nonChristian about the love of Christ. I think so.

IN ACTION: Some of our newspaper team people have a particular heart to reach out to those who ride buses, so they set up their newspaper posts at bus stops. When the bus pulls in to the stop, team members step onto the bus momentarily to see who would like the morning paper. As long as we're fast, the bus drivers love it.

IN ACTION: You never know who you're going to run into when you step out to do a small thing for someone in Christ's name. One pastor, who visited from out of state to see how we do outreach, went out with a small group to give away newspapers at a busy corner in urban Cincinnati. As he was distributing papers, a man he approached was someone he had been seeking to lead to Christ from his city hundreds of miles away. After he gave the shocked man a paper, he set up a lunch appointment for further conversation.

10 COFFEE/HOT CHOCOLATE/CAPPUCCINO GIVEAWAY

COFFEE, CAPPUCCINO, AND GOOD hot chocolate are all the rage these days; so wherever the chance presents itself, bring it to people during cooler months. On a blustery day, you can touch hundreds of shoppers as they go into a grocery store, for example, with the simple question, "Which would you like—a coffee or a hot chocolate? It's free!"

You need to have at least two options available: a coffee container and one for hot chocolate. A third container to add for the not-so-nervous group is decaf.

A more efficient but expensive route is to purchase a coffee backpack (available at www.servantevangelism.com). It has a hose on the side with an on-off valve for pouring coffee from the five-gallon container on the back. This may sound odd, but it's a quick way to give away a lot of hot chocolate or coffee.

You can use regular Styrofoam cups. Or add some style for just a little more money by having your church's logo imprinted on the sides of the cups. To do this, you need to order a significant number—certainly more than a small group could afford. But if several groups in your church are interested in doing something, they can work together on this.

Where to Go

- Campuses
- Parks
- Neighborhoods
- Sporting Events
- Downtown
- Commuters
- Shopping Centers

What You'll Need

- ☐ Container
- ☐ Hot chocolate mix
- ☐ Cappuccino mix
- ☐ Cups
- ☐ Condiments (sugar, creamers, stirrers)
- ☐ Connection cards

For the coffee purist, using a cappuccino mix is unthinkable, but mixes that are pretty good can be purchased in bulk for a reasonable amount. The project then involves you bringing the hot water and mixing it in the cup right before giving it away to customers. Cappuccino sounds a little extravagant, but business people will be impressed.

Note: Don't set up a coffee or cappuccino giveaway near a downtown coffee business. They won't experience much of God's love if you're competing for their business.

11 STAMP GIVEAWAY IN FRONT OF POST OFFICE

SOMETIMES IT ISN'T THE size of the outreach gift that makes an impression, it's the effort and the timing—it's being at the right time and the right place with the right gift.

Set up a table by the front door of the post office with your sign unfurled. Ask, "Do you need one stamp or two?" Don't receive the mail; let them post it themselves. Receiving letters is taking responsibility for getting the letters to the right place at the right time; that's more responsibility than you want to take on.

This is a popular project on April 15, Tax Day. One church has had an outreach on April 15 for the past several years. Ours goes all out by providing several tables of cakes, with cappuccino machines humming along. It's a party-like atmosphere (as much as that's possible on Tax Day). We usually make it onto the local news as a bright spot on that not-so-cheery day for most people.

WHERE TO GO

• Campuses
• Neighborhoods
• Downtown

WHAT YOU'LL NEED

☐ Stamps
☐ Folding table
☐ Signs: "Free Stamps"
☐ Connection cards

Another approach is to set up when postage rates increase by a cent or two and people are queuing up in long lines to buy a few of the stamps to send their mail. Why not provide those stamps for the few days just after the price changes?

12 BUSINESS BLAST

THE COMIC STRIP *DILBERT* has captured the hearts of millions with comedy that makes fun of the corporate rat race. But beneath the laughing, there's a lot of tragic truth to *Dilbert*. For the most part, those who work in the business and retail sector are not having a good time at their forty-hour-per-week grind.

The pain workers are experiencing is an opportunity for an outreach called the Business Blast. Make up excuses for coming into the work environment to bring a little cheer in the form of a soft drink, candy, or flowers, and try to bring the love of Christ to those who are desperate for a little practical evidence of God.

While it can be difficult to get permission to serve the patrons of a business, you can serve the employees where you might otherwise be turned down. Say, "Today we're here to serve the servers. We know they are often overlooked. We would like to give this gift to them today to demonstrate a bit of the kindness of Christ."

There are certain times during the year when Business Blasts are not only allowed, but also received with great enthusiasm.

Christmas is a particularly rough season on retail workers, so the month leading up to it is a great time to focus on reaching out with chocolates to those people. My church's favorite item for the last few seasons has been red and green M&M's. We tell the workers, "These are energy pills to show you God's love!" They are amused and touched, some to the point of tears.

Other product giveaways that work well:

- hard candies
- flowers
- long-distance calling cards
- soft drinks
- free car washes (just for the employees)
- truffles

WHERE TO GO

- Downtown
- Shopping Centers

WHAT YOU'LL NEED

☐ Product to give away (candy, flowers, and so on)
☐ Canvas bags to carry the goods
☐ Connection cards

Just about any time is a good time to do a Business Blast, but here are particularly good excuses for reaching out:

- Secretaries Day
- Valentine's Day
- Easter
- St. Patrick's Day
- Independence Day

IN ACTION: More than once at a Business Blast we've gotten great favor from the boss who invited us into the inner workings of the business. We've been invited to the back room where the employees gather. Once while washing toilets, we were escorted back to the break room to explain our project. The boss said, "Hey, listen up everyone. This is Steve. He has something to say to us." Now that's an entry point!

13 GROCERY BAG PACKING
(2 PER CHECKOUT LANE)

SOME PEOPLE HAVE COMMENTED that this project reminds them of the good old days of grocery store service when a high school kid was there just to help shoppers out to their cars.

At many large discount grocers you can save a few dollars a bag by buying in bulk; but when you check out, it's strictly bag-your-own. Contact the store manager a few days in advance of your project with an explanation. You want to provide help to shoppers with your bagging team. Each team member wears a "Kindness in Progress" vest. After asking, "Paper or plastic?" offer the customer a connection card to explain the project. Explain to all customers who you are and what you are doing so they don't assume you're part of the store's personnel.

WHERE TO GO

• Downtown
• Shopping Centers

WHAT YOU'LL NEED

☐ "Kindness in Progress" vests
☐ Connection cards

Make sure you do a high-quality job of packing by putting the heavy items (cans) on the bottom and the lighter or fragile items (bread, produce) on top. You'll get the hang of bagging pretty quickly.

Place a couple of baggers at each checkout lane, and the bagging goes very quickly.

IN ACTION: We have a great time talking to the checkout personnel. We become a sort of combination paid and volunteer team together. They are always very appreciative of our service. After a while, we develop relationships with these cashiers as we get to know them on a first-name basis.

14 GROCERY CART ESCORT AND RETURN

ON BUSY SATURDAYS, MOST grocery store parking lots have carts scattered throughout. The store needs the carts, but they're so busy inside they don't have time to run out to get them. As one who has worked at a grocery store, I know from experience that those who work in that environment are hurried from the moment they arrive until they clock out. Grocery store personnel will gladly receive your offer to help gather scattered carts.

This project goes well with the bag packing outreach at the same store. Your team does the necessary but irritating work of retrieving the carts from the parking lot. Wear your "Kindness in Progress" vests.

Hand out connection cards to the customers as well as to the employees. Shoppers will greatly appreciate your service.

We've found that larger grocery chains are more likely to reject this project due to store policy, fear of litigation, and other reasons. Go to local food chains or to a store where you have a relationship with the store manager.

As you explain your project to customers, make sure you're clear that you don't work for the grocery store. Even though you're wearing a vest that explains your project, people still need to be told.

Be open to praying for people you are serving. Some will be touched by your gift

WHERE TO GO

- Downtown
- Shopping Centers

WHAT YOU'LL NEED

- ☐ Connection cards
- ☐ "Kindness in Progress" vests

of service to the point that they will be open to sharing a prayer request if you offer, "Is there anything I can pray about for you?" Obviously you need to be sensitive. It only takes one complaint from a customer to be uninvited from the grocery store. However, we've had many prayer-sharing conversations in parking lots around the city with people whose hearts were opened by simple acts of serving.

15 POPSICLES/ICE CREAM GIVEAWAY
(5+ PER TEAM)

I REMEMBER AS A child the excitement of hearing the music of an ice cream truck when it was a couple of blocks away. That music was my cue to run to Mom to get some change for a treat. In Cincinnati, we've taken that concept and spun it a bit to make it totally free. This is one of the least expensive and most welcomed projects by both children and adults.

Some of the lower-priced pops (the kind you freeze yourself) are as little as five cents each when purchased

WHERE TO GO

- Campuses
- Parks
- Neighborhoods
- Sporting Events
- Downtown
- Commuters
- Shopping Centers

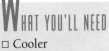**W**HAT YOU'LL NEED

- ☐ Cooler
- ☐ Dry ice
- ☐ Gloves (if you are going to handle the dry ice at all)
- ☐ Freezer pops
- ☐ Three or four signs: "Free Freezer Pops"
- ☐ Connection cards

in bulk. (Be aware: this type of treat takes several days to freeze sufficiently.)

Make sure to attach a card to these because in many cases you will be connecting with children without their parents.

You'll need a couple of Igloo-type ice chests with dry ice. The dry ice is a bit tricky to work with. Be sure to use leather gloves to avoid getting freezer burn.

IN ACTION: We've taken the original idea and run with it a bit by purchasing an ice cream truck. We even have speakers that play the music you heard as a kid that heralded the coming of the ice cream truck. With this we typically go to Kmart stores, Wal-Mart stores, soccer games, parks—anywhere families are gathered. We play our music and people come over to see what's going on. On the side of the truck we have the magnetic signs that say, "Free Popsicles!" We've also entered the truck in several parades. While others are just walking or riding in the parade, we are giving out treats to families all along the parade route.

Your small group probably can't afford its own ice cream truck, but you can make a less expensive alternative that would work well. Take a pickup truck, get some magnetic signs that read "Free Freezer Pops," put a boom box in the back with some kids' music, stock a couple of coolers with dry ice and a few hundred freezer pops, and you're ready to go. This truck approach works well on college campuses too. Students come out of the woodwork to get something for free.

16 ICE CREAM COUPONS
(5+ PER TEAM)

OF ALL THE GIVEAWAY projects our church has tried, I think nothing comes across as positively as ice cream coupons. Ice cream is a happy food. It's pretty much impossible to be bummed out and eat ice cream at the same time. When people eat it, they're usually thinking good thoughts. Because ice cream is a friendly food, the fact that you're giving it away conveys something positive to people.

Purchase ice cream certificates from local establishments. You'll likely get a discount if you shop around and explain to the suppliers what you are doing with the coupons. You can always go to McDonald's—they have good products and sell these certificates all the time. Chick-Fil-A restaurants also have great ice cream products at a good price.

Our favorite way of giving out the certificates is to go to movie openings. Our reasoning is that after the show the patrons will want to go out for a treat. As the long lines wind into the theater, moviegoers are open to receiving our free gift and even to talking a bit about why we are showing them this free gift of love. Be sure the ice cream store manager is aware of when you're doing the give-away so the store can be adequately staffed.

WHERE TO GO

- Campuses
- Parks
- Neighborhoods
- Sporting Events
- Downtown
- Commuters
- Shopping Centers

WHAT YOU'LL NEED

☐ Ice cream coupons
☐ Connection cards

IN ACTION: At one recent movie opening, a couple was approached: "Here's a free coupon for ice cream after the movie—just to show you God's love in a practical way." The gentleman said, "We don't eat ice cream, but what's this about God's love?" In the conversation that followed he said he had been touched by other acts of kindness by our church over the years in town and he was curious about why we did this. The conversation that followed continued all the while the line flowed into the theater.

17 HAND CLEANING TOWELETTES

HOW MANY TIMES A week are you somewhere and find your hands are dirty, but you can't get to a place to clean up? Some of those places are predictable (gas pumps, fairs, parades).

Individually wrapped towelettes are surprisingly inexpensive to have printed, but you will need to have several thousand printed initially. They look sharp with your church's name and phone number for as little as one cent per pack. We also include a connection card stapled to the actual towelette package.

Due to the printing cost, this is a project that will probably have to be done on a church-wide basis with several groups joining forces. Another less expensive option is to staple your connection card to a generic towelette package.

WHERE TO GO

- Campuses
- Parks
- Neighborhoods
- Sporting Events
- Downtown
- Commuters
- Shopping Centers

WHAT YOU'LL NEED

- ☐ Towelettes
- ☐ Connection cards
- ☐ Plexiglas holders (if you are going with self-service displays)

One great aspect of this project is that you can refill the container that holds the towelettes and it serves customers even when you aren't present. The towelettes give themselves away with your connection card attached. Some people in our church consider it their servant evangelism ministry to refill and pray over towelettes a couple of times a week.

 IN ACTION: At some gasoline stations we have set up self-serve towelette stations that are located either at the gas pumps or by the cash register inside the station. Station managers have been excited by the idea and gladly give away the towelettes for us. We have a Plexiglas container with a small sign that explains the project.

18 VINYL GLOVES AT GAS STATIONS

IN MOST AREAS, SELF-SERVICE gasoline stations are the norm for fueling automobiles. But there's some mess that comes with that. Often gasoline is on the pump handle when you pick it up, even if you don't spill any yourself. And the smell of gasoline is difficult to get off your skin.

WHERE TO GO

- Commuters

WHAT YOU'LL NEED

- ☐ Vinyl gloves
- ☐ Plexiglas holders
- ☐ Connection cards

Vinyl gloves are an inexpensive way to help motorists. Set up Plexiglas dispensers for the gloves at gas pumps or inside the stations at the cash register. Put together a connection card that reads, "Love gloves! This is to keep the gasoline off and protect your hands. It's our way of showing you God's love in a practical way. If we can be of more help, give us a call." This card is stapled to the wristband of each glove, and it's on a sign on the Plexiglas display.

The gloves cost only about five cents a pair.

19 WINDSHIELD WASHING
(5+ PER TEAM)

WHEREVER THERE ARE A lot of cars parked, like during Little League, soccer, or high school games, there are amazing opportunities just waiting for your group! This is a great project for touching a lot of people in a short time. A veteran washer can do thirty windshields in an hour.

Wash windshields by going from car to car. In Cincinnati, we do this without asking permission, but you might want to check with the city government where you live to make sure it's okay. This approach works well in middle-class parts of town where people view their cars as work tools. I don't recommend trying the phantom cleaning approach with nicer cars. Those who drive high-end cars may well like to have their windshields washed, but they don't want strangers touching their cars. Their preference is to drive to a washing station set up in a parking lot.

It isn't expensive to wash windshields once you've purchased the basics. Here are a few suggestions on what to use.

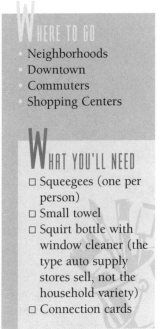

WHERE TO GO
- Neighborhoods
- Downtown
- Commuters
- Shopping Centers

WHAT YOU'LL NEED
- ☐ Squeegees (one per person)
- ☐ Small towel
- ☐ Squirt bottle with window cleaner (the type auto supply stores sell, not the household variety)
- ☐ Connection cards

- The best squeegees have a soft rubber edge on one side and a foam piece on the opposite; cost should be about five dollars. I recommend the ones with wooden handles; they allow you to press down more firmly on the window. When your squeegees are worn, toss them out.
- The standard red rags sold at auto parts stores work well as drying towels.
- I recommend you use the liquid window cleaner that is sold in auto parts stores rather than household types. The ammonia in some household cleaners can damage car paint.
- Use connection cards that are specially printed to explain your windshield-washing project. Ours read, "Your windshield looked a little dirty so we washed it! We hope this

small act of kindness brought light to your day. If we can be of more help, please give us a call." Put the card by the driver's-side handle, between the window and rubber seal, with the print facing out. Don't put it on the windshield. Cards on the windshield are usually overlooked and more irritating than thankfully received.

It takes a little practice to become proficient at window washing, but you can pick it up quickly after a car or two. (I recommend you practice on the cars in your own driveway first!)

To really clean a windshield, follow these steps:

- Thoroughly wet the foam piece of the squeegee. If the foam piece isn't wet, it won't scrub the window properly, especially if the weather is warm.
- Squirt the windshield wet with cleaning liquid.
- Run the foam side across the windshield to break up the dirt and debris.
- Starting at the top of the windshield, draw the squeegee toward you.
- Important: Dab the squeegee dry with your towel after each draw. A dry squeegee makes a clean swipe each time.
- When you get to the bottom, carefully lift the windshield wipers and clean under them. Be careful not to break or bend them. I've done both more than once. If you're careful, you shouldn't have any trouble. If you do break or bend a wiper, leave your name and number with a note of apology. Explain that you were doing a community service project and that the church will gladly pay for repairs. A wiper repair is a minimal expense—usually about twenty dollars.

IN ACTION: I've inadvertently set off a few car alarms, but remarkably, I've never had anyone get angry when they heard why I was doing this project. A friendly smile is powerful and disarming—even with a car alarm blaring! Smile, apologize, give the car owner the connection card, and tell him or her, "We're doing a community service project to show God's love in a practical way!" Most of the time, they'll understand.

20 PARKING METER FEEDING
(3+ PER TEAM)

FOR YEARS PEOPLE FROM my church have been giving a little relief to downtown shoppers by feeding their parking meters. No doubt your city or town has at least a few meters that require quarters and dimes. That is a great opportunity for outreach for your small group.

This outreach has undergone some changes over the years as local laws regarding meter feeding have changed. You might have read about the famous "Meter Feeding Granny" from Cincinnati who was arrested a few years ago for illegally feeding a meter. (Though she wasn't a member of our church, she was inspired by stories of our outreaches in downtown Cincinnati.) Early on with this project, we had inquired about the legality of feeding parking meters in Cincinnati, but had gotten mixed responses from the police—some said it was okay, others weren't sure. You'll be happy to hear that, since all of the media attention, we have revised the way we do this one and are now abiding by the letter of the law.

Before beginning to do this one I suggest you make a quick call to the local police department or city council offices to see what is technically legal.

Our new approach is to attach a coin to a special connection card. Use rubber cement—just enough to get the coin to stick, but not so much that it's difficult to pull off. Another way to connect the coin to the card is with a roller adhesive gun that lays down a thin layer of sticky substance on the card—just enough for a coin to attach. This product is available at office supply stores. This connection card reads, "It's Time for Some Change! Please use this coin to feed your next parking meter. This is a small way of saying, 'God loves you—no strings attached.' If we can be of more help, please give us a call." This approach lets the driver feed his or her own meter.

Take the cards with coins attached, place them in a carry bag,

WHERE TO GO
- Campuses
- Parks
- Neighborhoods
- Sporting Events
- Downtown
- Commuters
- Shopping Centers

WHAT YOU'LL NEED
- ☐ Quarters/dimes
- ☐ Removable adhesive
- ☐ Canvas bag for carrying your "loaded" cards
- ☐ Connection cards

and hit the streets. Pray for each car that you place a coin on. Slide the "loaded" card along the gap between the window and the rubber seal by the driver's door handle. Please don't put the card on the windshield. Many drivers will not notice it until they drive off. At that point, they will be irritated by your gesture. This is a great outreach for touching a lot of people (their cars, anyway) in a very short time. One meter feeder can make up to one hundred touches an hour.

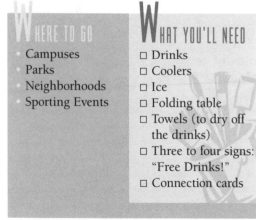 IN ACTION: Sometimes when I'm putting out these cards, homeless people follow me around and take the cards off as fast as I put them on the cars. When I see this happening I don't get mad (if I were homeless I might be tempted to do the same thing). Instead, I ask them how much money they expect to get from the quarters they are getting off the cars. Usually I suggest, "Why don't I just give you a few dollars for not taking the quarters off the cars. Do we have a deal?" They then leave the quarters alone.

21 DRINKS AT BIKING TRAILS

A LOT OF PEOPLE are health conscious these days. They converge regularly on parks and on running and biking trails to work out. Athletes are usually thirsty, but often they don't want soft drinks. Provide either water or sports drinks.

WHERE TO GO
- Campuses
- Parks
- Neighborhoods
- Sporting Events

WHAT YOU'LL NEED
- □ Drinks
- □ Coolers
- □ Ice
- □ Folding table
- □ Towels (to dry off the drinks)
- □ Three to four signs: "Free Drinks!"
- □ Connection cards

IN ACTION: A national sport-drink manufacturer heard what a small group at our church was doing at a bike trail and offered to sponsor their efforts. They supplied five thousand bottles of their product with no strings attached. We were happy to receive the free drinks; they were happy to be able to expose a lot of people to their new product.

22 PEN, PENCILS, AND POST-IT NOTES GIVEAWAY

REGISTRATION DAY AT THE beginning of the fall semester is a great time to connect with a lot of students. Specialty printers can put your church's name, phone number, and logo on pens and pencils for a few cents apiece. Post-It-type adhesive notes are popular as well. We've had these printed with our group's name, logo, and phone number on top. For a twenty-sheet three-inch-square tablet, the cost is about twenty cents. Each of these then becomes a sort of connection card in itself.

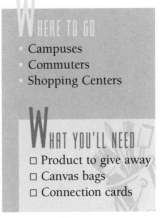

WHERE TO GO
- Campuses
- Commuters
- Shopping Centers

WHAT YOU'LL NEED
- ☐ Product to give away
- ☐ Canvas bags
- ☐ Connection cards

IN ACTION: At larger universities, all causes from wonderful to weird are represented at the central mall. I've seen a lot of different Christian groups try to connect in that setting, but one of the most effective approaches is the "Free Prayer" booth. Set up behind a folding table with a big sign, and staff your area with smiling, friendly, outgoing people. Most of those coming up will not actually ask for prayer. They will, however, be curious about your offer. When future difficulties come up, you'll find students turning to you for spiritual help.

23 PHOTOCOPYING

WHEN STUDENTS GO TO use the photocopier, they no longer put a coin in the machine; they slide in a prepaid card. Purchase cards that are worth fifteen to twenty copies per card to make your gift worth something to students. Imprint your church's information on the card so that it becomes your connection card.

WHERE TO GO
- Campuses

WHAT YOU'LL NEED
- ☐ Coupon cards

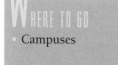

24 COMPUTER DISKETTES GIVEAWAY

FLOPPY DISKS ARE A staple of everyday school life. Purchase these in large quantities. Generic 3.5-inch disks are now about a dime apiece.

Place a sticker on these that lists your church's name and phone number. These can be given out door to door in the dorms or along with your pens and pencils during registration.

25 DRINKS AT INTRAMURAL OR GREEK EVENTS
(10+ PER TEAM)

NOT ALL GREEK EVENTS need to involve alcohol. Arrange in advance to provide the soft drinks or even mixed, nonalcoholic drinks for an event.

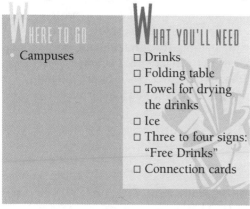

These days, many Greek organizations are trying to improve their public image and will jump at this chance. On top of good PR, drinks are served for free.

Make sure you have plenty of "designated evangelists" around to chat with the students to explain why you are doing this, to answer questions, and potentially to invite them to your group.

26 BREAKFAST TOASTER PASTRIES GIVEAWAY
(5+ PER TEAM)

TOASTER PASTRIES ARE INEXPENSIVE, and every college student seems to like them. Most students don't eat a proper breakfast, so you can provide it for them. They'll thank you and their mothers will thank you. Attach a connection card to the foil wrapper, or if you want to get a little fancier, set up a serv-ing stand in the stu-

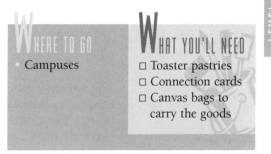

WHERE TO GO
• Campuses

WHAT YOU'LL NEED
☐ Toaster pastries
☐ Connection cards
☐ Canvas bags to carry the goods

dent center near an electrical outlet. Bring out your toasters and serve hot toaster pastries. You'll be famous all over campus in no time.

27 EXAM ANSWER (SCANTRON) SHEETS GIVEAWAY

IN MANY COLLEGE CLASSES, tests are administered with a stan-dardized multiple-choice exam sheet called a Scantron or bubble sheet. At midterms and finals, students can't take tests unless they bring their own answer sheets. These cost about a dime apiece. A couple of

WHERE TO GO
• Campuses

WHAT YOU'LL NEED
☐ Scantron sheets
☐ Connection cards

these attached to a connection card is a great, high-volume out-reach project.

 IN ACTION: Campus Crusade at Purdue University in Indiana caught on to the principles of servant evangel-ism and came up with the Scantron outreach a few years ago. One finals week, students were blitzing the campus with these answer sheets, when they came across what they describe as the "campus atheist" coming frantically out of one of his classes. You guessed it—he had forgotten to bring a Scantron sheet to his final exam and here he was, under the gun. A fresh-man girl felt a bit intimidated when she saw him, knowing how outspoken he was against the Christians on campus. With some fear and trembling, she handed him a Scantron. His response to the gift was "You don't know how meaningful this is to me. I won't forget it."

28 PHONE CARDS FOR LONG-DISTANCE CALLS
(5+ PER TEAM)

MANY PLACES SELL TEN or twenty minutes worth of long-distance time on prepaid phone cards, but have you ever received one for free? My church has given away five-minute phone cards for some years. With long-distance rates getting lower and lower, this is a better outreach deal all the time. You can even have the cards imprinted with your church's name, logo, and phone number.

WHERE TO GO
- Campuses
- Parks
- Neighborhoods
- Sporting Events
- Downtown
- Shopping Centers

WHAT YOU'LL NEED
□ Phone cards
□ Connection cards

We give these cards away in a variety of settings. One of our favorite places is on parade routes. We go to parades and enter with our own floats and give out the cards to people who are gathered on the street along the way.

IN ACTION: This is one of the most gratefully received gifts we've given away. It works especially well at significant holiday weekends, such as Mother's Day ("Here's a free card—you need to call your mom!").

For the cards our church gives away, the caller must dial a toll-free number and then punch in a unique code for the free phone time. When the user dials that toll-free number, a special recording explains in a professional phone voice, "You've reached the Vineyard Community Church's toll-free phone line. This call is provided free to show you God's love in a practical way. If we can be of more help, call us at 1.888.KINDNESS." In case they missed the original intent of the project, they get a second message with this recording.

29 "BIGGIE SIZE" FOOD ORDERS AT FAST FOOD DRIVE-THROUGHS
(3+ PER TEAM)

AT MANY FAST FOOD restaurants, you can purchase larger drinks and larger fries for thirty-nine cents more. (It's often called "biggie sizing" or "super sizing.") Set up at the drive-through lane just in front of the ordering menu microphone. Before people order, say, "Sir/Ma'am, could we biggie size that order for you?" With a connection card, hand them the exact change that is needed. The restaurant will be thrilled with your outreach (ask the manager for permission first, of course), because most of those pulling in decide to spend more money. You'll have a lot of brief conversations with car loads of people.

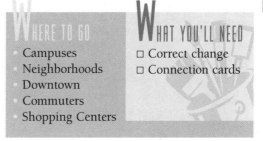

WHERE TO GO
- Campuses
- Neighborhoods
- Downtown
- Commuters
- Shopping Centers

WHAT YOU'LL NEED
- ☐ Correct change
- ☐ Connection cards

30 SUNTAN LOTION GIVEAWAY

IF YOUR COMMUNITY IS located near a beach, this is a project that is sure to succeed.

Suntan lotion is inexpensive when purchased in large quantities. (Don't actually apply the lotion! And it goes without saying: guys talk to guys, girls to girls. You want to avoid the appearance of evil.)

Offer lotion at different SPF strengths for those who are tanning at different levels.

You'll find that many already have suntan lotion, but this is a fantastic entry point for conversations with the beach crowd.

WHERE TO GO
- Parks

WHAT YOU'LL NEED
- ☐ Suntan lotion in several SPF strengths
- ☐ Connection cards

31 SURF WAX

THE SURFER COMMUNITY IS usually difficult to communicate with unless you are one of them. I've led outreach groups to surfers by meeting up with them at a practical level—by offering them something they need every time they hit the waves: surf wax. Before you buy any wax confer with some surfers to find out what brand is worth buying and what hardness is appropriate for the current weather conditions.

32 MOTHER'S DAY CARNATION GIVEAWAY
(5+ PER TEAM)

SOME PEOPLE FORGET OR wait until the last moment to get Mom a flower or card. Flowers can be expensive when purchased at the store individually, but they can be purchased for less than fifty cents per flower in bulk. Your group can probably explain to a local supermarket florist what you are trying to do with your outreach. Given enough advance notice, he or she can order a quantity of carnations and pass the discounted price on to you.

WHERE TO GO
- Campuses
- Parks
- Neighborhoods
- Sporting Events
- Downtown
- Commuters
- Shopping Centers

WHAT YOU'LL NEED
☐ Carnations
☐ Ribbons
☐ Connection cards

Attach to each flower a connection card and a ribbon. As with the soft drink giveaway, if you're doing this at the grocery store (where we usually locate), situate yourselves by the entrance, not the exit.

Another version of this is the Secretaries Day or Sweetest Day flower giveaway with a blank card for the giver to write his or her sentiments on as a greeting.

Don't give away flowers near a flower vendor.

33 CHURCH MATCH BOOK GIVEAWAY
(5+ PER TEAM)

THIS APPROACH MAY SOUND unorthodox, but it has worked famously for our outreaches in Cincinnati. Many smokers have an automatic assumption that church people dislike them or at least look down their noses at them. While we may not condone the smoking part,

I think it's safe to say that we love all people, smokers included. As an outreach to smokers, we've frequented restaurants, gasoline stations, convenience stores, and even bars with boxes of matches. These aren't just regular matches; they are church matches with our logo on the outside. Inside the cover, there's a map to our location, a list of service times, our phone number, and our website address.

WHERE TO GO
- Commuters
- Shopping Centers

WHAT YOU'LL NEED
☐ Custom-printed matches

Give these away with a little bit of shock value up front. I usually approach the manager of the establishment and say, "I'm giving away 'Christian' matches—they're free!" Of course, they've never heard of "Christian" matches, so a conversation follows. I end up explaining to them that these matches are for their smoking customers, to show them the love of Christ.

Matches are affordable once you get the initial printing done. The printing price is about five cents per pack. The packs themselves serve as connection cards.

34 WATERMELON/PUMPKIN/CANTALOUPE GIVEAWAY

WATERMELONS ARE PART OF what makes summer what it is, right? In the same way, pumpkins make fall. Go to local farmers and get a deal on a truckload of produce—usually for pennies on the dollar of what it would cost in the grocery store. Sometimes outreach leaders from my church have even received free fruit from farmers who heard about our outward vision.

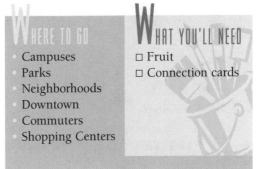

WHERE TO GO
- Campuses
- Parks
- Neighborhoods
- Downtown
- Commuters
- Shopping Centers

WHAT YOU'LL NEED
☐ Fruit
☐ Connection cards

Fill the back of a pickup with your melons and hit the streets. Drive through neighborhoods, knock on doors, and say to strangers,

"We're showing the love of Christ today by giving out these melons."
Give a connection card.

 IN ACTION: Something as simple as a watermelon may sound a little corny to some, but it gets the attention of the city. I met someone just the other day who said, "I'm at this church because someone gave me a watermelon two summers ago." It only takes a small thing to make a big impression sometimes.

35 BOXES TO MERCHANTS

CHRISTMAS, MOTHER'S DAY, VALENTINE'S Day, and Father's Day are all big retail sales days. For years, we've gotten our foot in the door with local merchants during holiday times. This is an especially welcomed outreach at chain stores that don't provide gift-wrapping—stores such as Target, Kmart, and Wal-Mart. Gift boxes are great for providing a practical help for customers and at the same time getting your name in many hands.

If you can't get into a place to do Christmas gift-wrapping (see pages 77-78), this is the next best approach. You can either give the boxes to merchants to distribute them, or give them out directly from an outreach booth in the front of the store. If you are using wrapping paper, place the connection stickers on the back of the gifts where the paper comes together. If you just use boxes and ribbons without paper, attach a sticker to one corner.

WHERE TO GO
- Shopping Centers

WHAT YOU'LL NEED
- ☐ Boxes in a variety of sizes
- ☐ Connection stickers with your church's information
- ☐ Connection cards

You need to order these boxes some months in advance of the event, especially if you are gearing up for Christmas. You will need several hundred per day of outreach at a good location.

36 SCOTCH TAPE GIVEAWAY AT CHRISTMAS

EVERYONE WRAPS PRESENTS AT Christmas, so everyone needs tape. Right? As shoppers come out of the store with presents in hand,

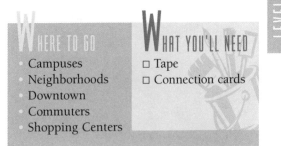

offer them tape with a connection card. For the past few years around Christmas, my church has purchased hundreds of rolls of tape and given them out to overwhelmed customers.

Where to Go
- Campuses
- Neighborhoods
- Downtown
- Commuters
- Shopping Centers

What You'll Need
- ☐ Tape
- ☐ Connection cards

It's amazing how many shoppers forget to buy the tape. We attach a connection card and offer them a little bit of holiday encouragement on their way to the car.

37 FLOWER SEED PACKET GIVEAWAY
(5+ PER TEAM)

WHO DOESN'T LIKE TO see flowers growing in their front yard? Do this project at fairs, carnivals, soccer games—literally anywhere crowds gather during the spring.

This is such a popular project that we are nearly mobbed by the takers. Carry big bags full of seed packets with connection cards stapled to them. Because we purchase these in large

Where to Go
- Campuses
- Parks
- Neighborhoods
- Sporting Events
- Downtown
- Commuters
- Shopping Centers

What You'll Need
- ☐ Seed packets
- ☐ Canvas bags to carry your seeds
- ☐ Connection cards

numbers, the seed companies print our church's name, logo, and phone number right on the seed pack.

We usually give away either marigold or pansy seeds. These are easy to successfully plant and grow, and they are rather inexpensive.

Seeds cost about five cents per pack when purchased in bulk.

38 GOLF TEE OR GOLF BALL GIVEAWAY, OR GOLF BALL CLEANING

GOLF TEES ARE INEXPENSIVE. Balls can be purchased in bulk with your name imprinted for less than one dollar. Put several tees in small zip-close plastic bags with a connection card. Do the same with golf balls. Offer them to golfers at either the pro shop or at golf ball cleaning stations. Because pro shops sell these items, you will need to make arrangements with the golf pro in advance. Suggest a two-hour "Kindness Morning to Golfers" outreach on a Saturday morning. This is a great men's ministry outreach.

WHERE TO GO

- Parks
- Sporting Events

WHAT YOU'LL NEED

☐ Materials for giving away
☐ Connection cards

When purchasing tees, you have the choice of what you want printed on them. Knowing the ups and downs of golf as I do, I recommend using the phrase "The best is yet to come." Golfers will find that humorous and memorable.

39 GLOW-IN-THE-DARK NECKLACE GIVEAWAY

PERHAPS YOU'VE SEEN THESE neon necklaces at amusement parks; they have a chemical substance that makes them glow brightly for a few hours. Buy a hundred at a time to get a good price; each necklace runs about a dollar. If you have some money saved up in the outreach fund, this is a good one on a warm summer night. You'll get a lot of attention—

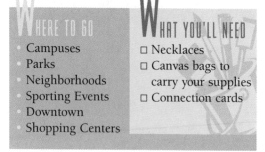

WHERE TO GO

- Campuses
- Parks
- Neighborhoods
- Sporting Events
- Downtown
- Shopping Centers

WHAT YOU'LL NEED

☐ Necklaces
☐ Canvas bags to carry your supplies
☐ Connection cards

in fact the crowds may mob you. Of course, most of those wanting a necklace will be children or teenagers. Give the necklaces to the parents of younger children first, and let them give them to their kids. This approach will also allow you to have at least a passing conversation with the parents about the project.

Hole punch the connection card and slip the necklace through it.

LEVEL 2
CONNECTING TO THE COMMUNITY

THESE PROJECTS GIVE THE opportunity for greater interaction with people in your community and a greater chance for more-significant conversation. You may not make as many "touches" as with blitzing approaches, but the connections you do make will tend to spin off deeper conversations and, therefore, open greater doors to share the gospel.

Connecting projects are great for the following:

- providing a safe place for *experimenting* with outreach
- a chance to truly *serve* the public (With the blitzing approaches, your group does a lot of generous giving away of products, but not a lot of giving away of time. More than things, people love the gift of time when it is given.)
- an opportunity to get into significant and evangelistic *conversations* with those being served
- a great place for families with young *children* to get involved with outreach ministry
- a chance to develop *humble hearts*

40 TOTALLY FREE CAR WASH
(12+ PER TEAM)

WE'VE ALL HEARD OF the so-called free car wash sponsored by church youth groups, but usually it entails a donation at the end. Not so with this one. Get big banners that read, "Free Car Wash—No Kidding!" Our hand-held signs read, "No Donations Accepted!" and "Totally Free Car Wash." The word "free" intrigues people. Use it and make them wonder.

Though this will not generate the number of contacts other projects will, it is fairly foolproof and it provides the opportunity to have some in-depth conversations with motorists.

Set up on a street that has a significant traffic flow at a location

WHERE TO GO

- Campuses
- Parks
- Neighborhoods
- Downtown
- Commuters
- Shopping Centers

WHAT YOU'LL NEED

- ☐ Five or six signs: "Totally Free Car Wash," "Free Car Wash—No Kidding!" and "No Donations Accepted!"
- ☐ Six buckets
- ☐ Dawn dishwashing soap (works great for cars)
- ☐ "Y" hose splitters
- ☐ Two sections of thirty-foot garden hose
- ☐ Towels for drying (optional)
- ☐ Squeegees
- ☐ Wheel-cleaning brushes
- ☐ Boom box with nice music
- ☐ Soft drinks for servants and those served as you wash
- ☐ Connection cards

with an easy entrance and exit. You'll need plenty of water—hopefully you will be able to have access to two or more faucets.

A successful car wash needs two things: great signs and a rapid flow of traffic. Get the attention of motorists. Place several high-energy, cheerleader types on corners near your site. Tell them to shake their signs, whistle, wave their hands, and generally direct people into the wash.

You need a minimum of twelve to fifteen people to do this project, so if your group is smaller than that, you might consider teaming up with another group on this one.

Divide your labor force into categories for efficient serving. Have a rinsing team, washing team, tire team, and drying team (drying is an option depending on the weather conditions and traffic flow). When the traffic begins to really pick up, you will want to have several parallel lanes of washing going at once.

Sometimes you will get so busy washing that those being served won't get a clear explanation of the project. It's vital, therefore, to assign one or two designated evangelists to do the explaining to motorists.

If you want to get fancy, provide lawn chairs for people to sit on as well as cold drinks. We sometimes have Christian music playing to help create a positive atmosphere. As we wash their cars, it's only natural to share the hope that lies within us and to offer to pray for needs people may have.

 IN ACTION: Car washes are great places for kids to get involved in servant evangelism. About the only thing they can't do well is the rinsing. My son, Jack, is an enthusiastic nine-year-old. Out of our church of several thousand, Jack is arguably one of the best sign people. When he helps flag people into the car wash, we get so much business we sometimes have to get him to take a break!

IN ACTION: The best cars are usually the last ones to pull in. Be open to washing those cars that pull up just as you are getting ready to quit and are rolling up the hoses. Sometimes those are the best contacts of the day. These latecomers are the taxed-out people who drove by earlier but were in a hurry to get somewhere else. They did their errands, and now they're swinging back by the free car wash—but a little frayed around the edges. Often these people are open and receptive to conversation about Christ—and even about receiving prayer.

41 INTERIOR CAR CLEANING AND VACUUMING

AFTER DOING FREE CAR washes for more than a decade, I've found that many people would rather have the inside of their car cleaned than the outside.

As with the car wash, you'll need several large signs to draw attention. Remember, when doing most of these projects you can't have too many signs!

Bring a number of vacuum cleaners with a lot of extension cords.

Do the windows while you're at it. Even when cars are washed on the outside, grime on the inside usually doesn't get touched. If you get the inside windows sparkling, you'll

WHERE TO GO

- Campuses
- Parks
- Neighborhoods
- Sporting Events
- Downtown
- Commuters
- Shopping Centers

WHAT YOU'LL NEED

- ☐ Two to four Shop-Vac-type vacuum cleaners
- ☐ Electrical source with enough amperage to support that many vacs
- ☐ Extension cords
- ☐ Three to four signs: "Free Car Vacuuming"
- ☐ Sachets (optional)
- ☐ Armor All (optional)
- ☐ Connection cards

be remembered for weeks to come. When finished, place a sachet in the car as a nice extra touch.

You can apply a coat of Armor All to the vinyl for just a few pennies per car. This entire outreach is close to what someone would get with a high-priced, detailed interior car wash that would cost twenty dollars—a nice gift.

Of course, while the cleaners are doing their job, designated evangelists need to be talking to the car owners.

42 OIL CHANGES FOR SINGLE PARENTS

THIS IS A GREAT project for involving mechanically inclined group members on a Saturday morning in reaching out to some of God's favorite people. With a bit of teamwork you can provide an oil change, a new oil filter, and a topping off of windshield washer liquid.

WHERE TO GO

- Campuses
- Parks
- Neighborhoods
- Downtown

WHAT YOU'LL NEED

- ☐ Scooters (for getting under cars)
- ☐ Oil pans
- ☐ Waste oil container
- ☐ Motor oil appropriate for the season
- ☐ Oil filter wrench
- ☐ Array of commonly used filters
- ☐ Connection cards

You'll need to know the make and model of the car in advance in order to purchase the correct oil filters. I suggest you go door to door in an apartment complex where lots of single parents live. If they need your service, give them a scheduled time and date for the oil change. Start this project within your congregation and expand from there. The first time or two of doing this you may have a low turnout, but the news of your generosity will spread. There's a big, caring network in the single-parent community.

Offer to pray for the moms or dads as they are having their cars worked on.

A word of caution: You'll be asked to do more repairs on cars than the oil change. Stay away from getting in too deep. Your goal is to keep doing this outreach for some time to come. To avoid a case of compassion fatigue, start small and build your outreach gradually and as a group. Some individuals within your group with the gift of mercy will be drawn to either pay for car repairs or to take on the responsibility to fix cars themselves. Resist that temptation. It's absolutely fine to tell those being served, "All we are doing is the following. . . . Maybe someday we'll be doing more, but not today." Then smile, and change the oil of the next car in line.

43 CAR DRYING AT SELF-SERVE CAR WASHES
(6+ PER TEAM)

PICTURE THIS: AS WET cars pull out of self-serve washing stalls, a small army of towel-carrying servants descends to dry them.

You'll seldom be turned down with this offer. Those with nicer, more-expensive cars may turn you down, but as with all the projects, it's the offer that counts.

Be sure to have enough designated evangelists—I recommend three to five at a busy car wash. There will be plenty of opportunities for conversation with this one.

You will run out of dry towels pretty quickly, so bring plenty. Another approach is to use leather chamois to dry the vehicles as they come out. These can be wrung out as they become wet.

WHERE TO GO
- Commuters

WHAT YOU'LL NEED
- ☐ Towels or chamois
- ☐ Connection cards

44 WINDSHIELD WASHER FLUID FILL

TYPICAL WINTER OR SPRING driving—through puddles, mud, and slush—quickly covers windshields with a layer of goo. Drivers need a regular refill of the blue stuff. Set up a refill station in a visible corner of a grocery store, mall parking lot, or gas station. You'll need several large signs (I prefer banners) that read something like "Free Windshield Washer Refills!" If you want to get fancy, you can also replace windshield wiper blades (you'll need to purchase a variety of common sizes).

A note to be aware of on this project: make sure you refill the washer fluid reservoir (blue liquid) and not the radiator fluid reservoir (yellow liquid). A group from my church made that costly mistake! The two chemicals don't mix well. (We had to foot the bill to have the radiator flushed.)

WHERE TO GO
- Commuters
- Shopping Centers

WHAT YOU'LL NEED
- ☐ Windshield washer fluid
- ☐ Connection cards

45 WINDSHIELD ICE SCRAPING

IN MUCH OF THE country, cars left outside at night are prone to frost for about half the year. It's a hassle to scrape your own car when you're in a hurry to get to work.

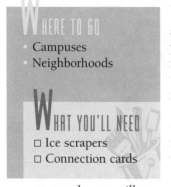

WHERE TO GO

• Campuses
• Neighborhoods

WHAT YOU'LL NEED

☐ Ice scrapers
☐ Connection cards

Once you're out in the cold, it's just as easy to do five or ten cars as it is to do your own car. Get up a littler earlier and move down the parking lot or street. Do the same thing after work for people commuting home.

When finished, place a contact card by the driver's-side door handle. (Remember, it's irritating to have something stuck under the windshield wiper.)

Because you are doing this outreach to people you will see regularly (either coworkers or neighbors), pray as you scrape—pray for the progression of each person you serve, that they will move closer to receiving Christ. You'll be somewhat under the microscope once you begin to do these projects in close quarters. Pray for grace and favor and strength to be consistent in your witness. God will make you able.

46 WINDSHIELD WASHING AT SELF-SERVE GAS STATIONS

IN THE DAYS OF full service gas stations, a motorist had his or her windshield washed with each fill up. It's not so in these days of self-serve gasoline. On Saturday mornings, invade gas stations with squeegees, squirt bottles, drying rags, and connection cards to serve (see page 48 for how to properly use a squeegee). This project is a step beyond the one outlined earlier because you will be

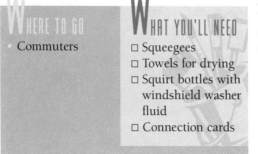

WHERE TO GO

• Commuters

WHAT YOU'LL NEED

☐ Squeegees
☐ Towels for drying
☐ Squirt bottles with windshield washer fluid
☐ Connection cards

interacting with those you are serving. As their cars are being refueled and as you wash their windshields, they'll be conversing with you.

As drivers pull in for gas, say, "Hi, we're washing windshields today to show customers the love of Christ. How about if I do yours?!" Give them a connection card. Make sure you clarify that you are not a part of the gasoline station personnel (they will automatically think you are if you don't make that distinction). Explain that you are there to show the love of Christ in a practical way.

You'll find some resistance from chain stations for fear of possible lawsuits. We carry insurance for this very reason, but it will still be difficult to convince most managers. Don't give up! There are always locally owned, nonchain stations that will be willing to work with you.

47 BIKE FIX-UP CLINIC

THOSE NEEDING BIKE REPAIRS are mostly kids with their parents. So, while this outreach is aimed at the child with the bike, your conversation will be with the parents while the repairs are taking place. In addition to the repair tools, you will need connection cards and a few designated evangelists to connect with the crowd.

We set up signs that advertise our project, and we go to three places:

1. grocery stores (kids riding their bikes up from the neighborhood; we also pass out flyers at the exit doors to customers so they can go home and bring back their bikes)
2. bike trails (kids with their parents)
3. Matthew's Party (as part of the total excitement of the event; see pages 92-93 for more information on this outreach)

Define what repairs you will be doing. We mostly do chain repairs and lubes, spoke repairs, bolt tightening, and simple cable adjustments on gearshifts and brakes. Bike mechanics' lifts make

WHERE TO GO
- Campuses
- Parks
- Neighborhoods
- Sporting Events
- Downtown
- Commuters
- Shopping Centers

WHAT YOU'LL NEED
☐ Two signs: "Free Bike Repair"
☐ Repair tools (informed repair people will know what to bring along)
☐ Connection cards

this project much easier on the backs of those doing the work and make the project look a lot more professional.

48 RESTROOM CLEANING

THIS IS THE MOST radical of all the projects. More heads will turn and more mouths will drop when you offer to clean someone's toilets than with any other project. Go into gasoline stations, restaurants, convenience stores, and even bars to offer this service. It's best to go for a little bit of shock value with this. With cleaning kit in hand, approach the manager, hand him or her a connection card, and say, "Hi, we'd like to clean your toilets for free!" Often the managers are so shocked at the offer they'll ask, "Could you repeat that? It sounded like you said you wanted to clean our toilets!" Everyone in the establishment who hears this will be drawn into the conversation.

WHERE TO GO
- Neighborhoods
- Sporting Events
- Downtown
- Shopping Centers

WHAT YOU'LL NEED
- ☐ Plastic caddy (the kind that has a dividing wall in the middle to separate the wet from the dry cleaning tools)
- ☐ Kit contents: Window cleaner, porcelain cleaner, paper towels, toilet bowl cleaner, toilet brush, deodorizer, doorstop, rubber gloves, light bulbs
- ☐ Connection cards

Put together a cleaning kit. Purchase the plastic caddy at a janitorial supply company or at a Kmart or other discount store. This caddy needs to have two sections separating the dry materials from the wet ones. Stock the kit with the contents listed to the left. Have one kit per two people. Have a guy and a girl on each team—guys do the men's restrooms, girls do the girls.

To avoid surprising anyone, prop the door open with the doorstop. Then spray the air with the deodorizer. Clean the mirrors first, then the porcelain. Be sure you don't mix these chemicals—poisonous gas can form if you do. Clean as quickly as possible. Don't get hung up on a perfect job or you'll be there for longer than is appropriate. When you're finished, put several connection cards on the back of the toilet. Finally, before leaving, tell the manager you're done, and that it's been a pleasure serving his or her business.

IN ACTION: We've even gone beyond just cleaning toilets to getting our own urinal screens printed with our church's name and phone number on it. (No kidding! For a sample, give us a call at 1-888-KINDNESS, or contact us at www.servant-evangelism.com, and we'll send you one.)

This project is perhaps the most shocking of all and, therefore, is about the most often denied when we ask permission to do it. I'm pretty convincing in my approach to managers, and I have been turned down plenty of times. I've kept a running log of the most common reasons why people don't want their toilets cleaned (they're mostly made up, I suspect):

- "We just cleaned them five minutes ago!"
- "Gee, I better not let you [thumbing through the policy manual]. I can't find any specific company policy on this."
- "Our toilet is so filthy I'm embarrassed for you to see it!" (We cleaned it anyway. They were right—it was pretty bad.)
- "Are you sure you want to clean it? This is a joke right? Are you guys from *Candid Camera* or something?"

49 UMBRELLAS ESCORT

ON DREARY, RAINY DAYS there's nothing like a little encouragement to lift your spirits. Merchants will love this effort.

Gather your spare umbrellas—the bigger, the better—and head out to the local grocery store or shopping center on a rainy day. Wait by the exit areas for shoppers coming out laden with bags of goods. Most shoppers, even if they have an umbrella, can't hold it and push their carts at the same time. If they're parents, they're dealing with one or more children and the rain.

As shoppers come

WHERE TO GO

- Campuses
- Parks
- Neighborhoods
- Sporting Events
- Downtown
- Commuters
- Shopping Centers

WHAT YOU'LL NEED

- ☐ Large umbrellas (two per team member—one for the member and one for those he or she serves)
- ☐ "Kindness in Progress" vests
- ☐ Connection cards

out of the store, step forward with your umbrella and say, "We're the umbrella escort team!" Stroll along and explain that you are not from the store, but that you are doing this to show the love of God in a practical way to shoppers. As usual, give them a connection card. Once you get to the car, offer to help them unload their groceries.

If you do this project regularly, invest in some golf umbrellas (they are oversized and colorful). They're not much of an investment—usually less than ten dollars.

50 NEIGHBORHOOD FOOD COLLECTION AND DISTRIBUTION

THESE DAYS, THE GENERAL public is interested in giving to the needy. There's a desire in the hearts of many suburban people to do more than observe ministry to the poor—they want to be personally involved. This is a project that can get your entire neighborhood involved.

Go door to door to collect canned goods and then give those goods to the needy at an upcoming Matthew's Party (see pages 92-93 for details on how that is run). Knock on doors in the neighborhood where the small group meets and say, "Hi, I'm from a small group that meets in this neighborhood. We are collecting canned goods in this neighborhood today. We've already gotten food from _____ down the street. We're going to have a party for the needy where we will be giving this food away. If you're interested, we'd be happy to give a few canned items to the needy in our city on your behalf."

WHERE TO GO
- Campuses
- Parks
- Neighborhoods
- Downtown
- Commuters
- Shopping Centers

WHAT YOU'LL NEED
☐ Paper or plastic bags
☐ Connection cards

You will get food from nearly 100 percent of those you approach. You might get a few people who are interested in checking out your small group; they're going to be curious about any group that is interested in the poor. Give each household a connection card.

On the first time around the neighborhood, don't do much more than what is outlined above, but on the second time, when there's a bit more rapport, ask them if there is anything you can pray about for them. Give them the time and place of the upcoming Matthew's Party. These parties are extremely safe and approachable—even for complete strangers. Your neighbors will be very positively touched if they come.

51 BUSINESS WINDOW WASHING

INVEST A LITTLE IN some good equipment and do a good, streak-free job (see page 48 on how to use a squeegee). You will need a rectangular bucket, cleaning liquid, a lamb's wool cleaning head, and a wide squeegee. All of these items can be purchased at a janitorial supply store.

After you get the hang of using a squeegee, you can do a front window and door in about five minutes. The manager will be impressed and will usually be open to talking in more depth when you're done. Leave a connection card. If you have a sense of God's calling to a particular part of town, return there repeatedly, and gradually build a relationship with the workers around there. It will only be natural to offer prayer as you get to know them.

WHERE TO GO

- Campuses
- Neighborhoods
- Sporting Events
- Downtown
- Shopping Centers

WHAT YOU'LL NEED

- ☐ Squeegees (those sold in auto supply stores will do, but I recommend the higher quality brass versions sold at janitorial supply stores)
- ☐ Lamb's wool window scrubbers
- ☐ Rectangular plastic buckets (to fit the shape of the squeegees)
- ☐ Cleaning formula (available at janitorial supply stores)
- ☐ Connection cards

52 POLAROID PHOTOS

WE'VE HAD GREAT success tying this outreach to a seasonal event like Easter, Christmas, or Mother's Day.

Instant photos are affordable when the film is purchased in bulk.

WHERE TO GO

- Campuses
- Parks
- Neighborhoods
- Sporting Events
- Downtown
- Commuters
- Shopping Centers

WHAT YOU'LL NEED

□ Polaroid cameras (one camera per team of three to four people)
□ Plenty of film (four to six rolls per camera will last about two hours at a good location)
□ Connection cards or stickers

Find someone to do the shooting who has an eye for portrait photos. We place the photos inside matte frames that are color-coordinated to go with the season. Place a sticker with your group or church's name on the back of it. Sometimes a local mall has paid the entire bill for the film and matte frames because it brought in a significant flow of shopper traffic.

Because of that traffic, be sure that in addition to the photographers and crowd control people you have a number of designated evangelists to explain your project to the families who are gathered. Bring a lot of connection cards.

53 SHOESHINES

THERE'S NOTHING LIKE A shoeshine to make a person feel on top of the world. This project works particularly well in an urban area, but you'll get some attention from suburbanites as well. You'll also have plenty of opportunity to talk while shining.

WHERE TO GO

- Campuses
- Parks
- Neighborhoods
- Sporting Events
- Downtown
- Commuters
- Shopping Centers

WHAT YOU'LL NEED

□ Shoeshine kit (polish, brushes)
□ Sign: "Free Shoeshine"
□ Connection cards

Put together a basic kit. Find a place with some decent foot traffic. A grocery store is a great place to set up operations.

Don't offer shoeshines near someone else who is doing this as a business.

IN ACTION: A small group outside of Amsterdam has a heart to reach out to the gothic youth of their city. They've taken the shoeshine project one step further: they touch up black leather coats, pants—you name it.

54 HELIUM BALLOONS AND BALLOON ANIMALS

GO TO PARKS, GROCERY store exits, fairs, and parades with balloons and you'll draw a crowd quickly. Buy helium from a local distributor and they'll probably let you use the dolly and tank for free. One large tank will fill about 250 balloons. Attach a connection card to each balloon string. Tell the children they need to have their parents come with them to get the balloon—this is to avoid giving multiple balloons to each child and also to give you a chance to explain to the parents what you're doing.

A second version of this project is a balloon animal outreach. Purchase balloon pumps and a few hundred of the long, thin balloons, then do some practice sessions. Find someone who is able to show your group how to make five or six basic animals. Once you get the hang of it, these are easy to make and kids will be amazed. As you make the balloons, explain to the parents why you are doing this outreach.

WHERE TO GO

- Campuses
- Parks
- Neighborhoods
- Sporting Events
- Downtown
- Shopping Centers

WHAT YOU'LL NEED

☐ Nine-inch balloons (250 per large helium tank)
☐ Helium tank(s)
☐ Dolly for the tank(s)
☐ String for the balloons
☐ Scissors
☐ "Animal" balloons
☐ Pump for thin balloons
☐ Sign: "Totally Free Balloons"
☐ Connection cards

55 DOG WASHING
(5+ PER TEAM)

THIS PROJECT WILL GET the attention of your neighborhood in a hurry. After all, how often does someone come to your door and offer to

WHERE TO GO

- Campuses
- Parks
- Neighborhoods
- Downtown
- Shopping Centers

WHAT YOU'LL NEED

☐ Hoses
☐ Dog shampoo
☐ Towels
☐ Tank
☐ Flea collars (optional)
☐ Connection cards

wash your dog for free?

If you are looking for an entry point into an upper middle-class neighborhood but can't get in the front door, you might stoop down to the doggie door. When people are closed off to connecting directly at a one-to-one level, they'll talk to you over the safe subject of their pet.

All you need is a big tank, some shampoo, a hose, and some drying towels. Do the actual washing at the curb near a drain. Don't use human shampoo; it dries out a dog's coat. Pick up a big bottle of pet shampoo at the pet store. If you want to be fancy, you can put ribbons in their hair, paint their nails—get creative.

Set up operations centrally in a neighborhood and invite people to come to you at a specific time. Run your dog wash for a couple of hours from a set time.

People really connect and open up to strangers over the topic of their pets. We've found that when we show kindness to Fido, we are also showing great kindness to Fido's owner. Be sure to have a couple of designated evangelists who are not washing, but explaining the reason for the pet wash. Be ready for entire families to come out on this one.

A nice touch after the wash: give the dogs a biscuit. The owners will be thrilled. A flea collar is a nice option as well.

Because this is done in a neighborhood setting, it's a great entry point into the area where your small group regularly meets. This outreach can be done in about any setting—urban or suburban.

IN ACTION: Two ten-year-old boys came up with this project. They went out a weekend in advance with a flyer that was a takeoff of the inscription at the base of the Statue of Liberty: "Bring us your tired, your dingy, your dirty, your dogs yearning to breathe free air." These flyers were printed with the dog wash time and location and taken door to door in the neighborhood. The results? As they reported it to me, "A lot of conversations with the owners of fifteen dogs."

56 DOGGIE DIRT CLEANUP

SET UP A SIGN, "Doggie Dirt Patrol," and go door to door in neighborhoods. I guarantee that your neighborhood will be blown away at your offer to clean up dog droppings. They may deny you permission out of their surprise, but they'll never forget your offer! No matter how much business you get, you'll be involved in some great conversations with those you offer to serve. You are showing an extreme level of care when you show up with the "super duper scooper" in hand.

WHERE TO GO

- Parks
- Campuses
- Neighborhoods

WHAT YOU'LL NEED

- ☐ One doggie dirt scooper per team (can be purchased at a pet store; looks like a pair of tongs with metal fork hands)
- ☐ Plastic bags
- ☐ Gloves
- ☐ Sign: "Doggie Dirt Patrol"
- ☐ Connection cards

57 DORM MOVE-IN HELP

MOVING INTO A DORM as a freshman is overwhelming for most students—especially if their room is on the fourth floor! A couple of well-organized small groups will have their work cut out for them with this project, but they'll connect at a deep level with those they serve.

Look for students who appear to be stressed out as they unload their gear from the parking lot. Jump right in with an offer of help by saying, "We're here to bring your stuff to your room."

Team up with an on-campus group you feel good about, such as InterVarsity Christian Fellowship, so you can funnel students both to your local church and to the campus group. Keep in mind that the majority of

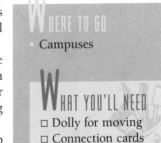

WHERE TO GO

- Campuses

WHAT YOU'LL NEED

- ☐ Dolly for moving
- ☐ Connection cards

students who come to Christ during college do so during their freshman and sophomore years. Take advantage of this positive vulnerability during the first part of their college experience.

We've had a hamburger cookout at the end of the move-in for everyone to connect over some food and drink. It's a great chance to talk and to invite students to your church or campus group.

58 COFFEE, TEA, AND LATTES DURING LATE-NIGHT STUDY SESSIONS

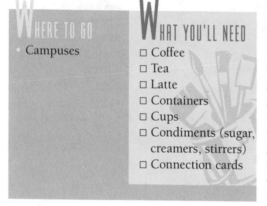

LOCATE THE STUDY AREAS on campus where students congregate during finals week and serve them highly caffeinated products. They'll often be in a bit of a hurry to get back to their studies, but short conversations will abound. Be open to getting prayer requests— no kidding. Just as there are no atheists in foxholes, there are none when it comes to finals time.

WHERE TO GO
- Campuses

WHAT YOU'LL NEED
- ☐ Coffee
- ☐ Tea
- ☐ Latte
- ☐ Containers
- ☐ Cups
- ☐ Condiments (sugar, creamers, stirrers)
- ☐ Connection cards

59 SOFT DRINKS, GATORADE, AND LEMONADE AT CLASS SIGN-UP

WHEN YOU WERE IN college, didn't it seem like the registration lines were always long and the weather was always unbearably hot? Set up some refreshment tables. This outreach is similar to the ones done at stop lights, but you'll have more chance to actually talk to people. Take advantage of the

WHERE TO GO
- Campuses

WHAT YOU'LL NEED
- ☐ Drinks
- ☐ Coolers
- ☐ Ice
- ☐ Folding table
- ☐ Towel
- ☐ Connection cards

open doors as they present themselves.

Keep in mind that most students, Christians included, never connect with a church or small group while they're in school. Give them such a positive impression that they'll want to connect with yours. Be friendly, be enthusiastic, be inviting.

Have plenty of connection cards.

60 PIZZA ON MOVE-IN DAY AT DORMS

PIZZA AND COLLEGE GO hand in hand. On the first day of school, get your foot in the door with everyone on a dorm floor with pizza.

Contact a local pizza business to get a quantity discount. Go door to door in the dorm. With each slice we give out a connection card and say, "Just want to welcome you.

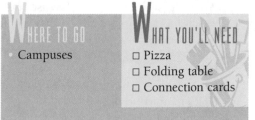

WHERE TO GO
• Campuses

WHAT YOU'LL NEED
☐ Pizza
☐ Folding table
☐ Connection cards

We're from the ____ small group. Here's our card."

61 CHRISTMAS GIFT-WRAPPING

IN ANY CITY, THE local mall is hands down the greatest place to connect with people. It's the modern-day town center where people from every socioeconomic stratum gather. However, most malls aren't open to Christians doing evangelistic outreaches, even those as simple as servant evangelism. Malls are sometimes fearful about liability issues or a community group already has its foot in the door. We've gotten around that by going to malls to offer them something they need during the Christmas season—gift-wrapping.

For more than ten years, my church has had great success at reaching a lot of people as we wrap their presents between Thanksgiving and Christmas Eve.

A good alternative to locating at the mall is a chain store like Sears, Target, Kmart, or Wal-Mart.

How long should the wrapping go on? I don't recommend starting off with more sessions than you can adequately handle. Our first attempt at this was manned by a number of small groups banding together over the several weeks between Thanksgiving and Christmas. We signed on to cover every day during those weeks. That turned out to be more than we could realistically take on. We pulled it off, but not without being stretched to the limit. During that first attempt at Christmas wrapping, we did touch a lot of people—we wrapped some ten thousand people's presents. And we had some amazing conversations.

Buy the gift-wrapping paper in bulk from a distributor to get the best prices.

We use "Bow Magic" bows (made by 3M). They go from flat to popped up when the end is pulled. They are well worth the cost of about ten cents apiece.

I recommend you do a practice session or two before beginning to wrap in earnest.

Where to go

- Campuses
- Downtown
- Shopping Centers

What you'll need

☐ Tape
☐ Wrapping paper (we usually buy it on rolls)
☐ Roll carousel
☐ Scissors
☐ Bows
☐ Folding tables (raise tables to waist height to avoid causing back problems as people stoop over to wrap)
☐ Post-It-type notes
☐ Pens
☐ Connection cards

IN ACTION: When wrapping presents, open up the conversation with those you're serving by saying, "You know, we aren't employees of the mall. We're here on our own. We bought and paid for all of these materials and we're doing it all for free to show you and the community the love of Christ for free at Christmas."

62 MEAL PURCHASING AT RESTAURANTS

YOU'LL GET THE ATTENTION of all the workers at the restaurant quickly with this outreach project.

Take a spontaneous offering within your group. Give that to the restaurant manager (we usually do this at a fast food place), explaining, "We'd like to pay for the next several customers' meals until the money runs out. Tell them this is from the people from _____ Church to show God's love in a practical way. We're sitting right over there if they'd like to talk to us." Give the manager a stack of connection cards to give out with your gift. Each time we've done this, we've had stunned restaurant personnel (word travels fast) as well as numbers of customers showing up to ask what's up with our project.

Set up at a table in the restaurant and wait for customers who want to discuss this further.

This outreach also works well at coffee shops where people tend to linger.

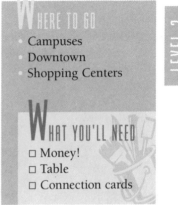
WHERE TO GO
- Campuses
- Downtown
- Shopping Centers

WHAT YOU'LL NEED
- □ Money!
- □ Table
- □ Connection cards

IN ACTION: I did this outreach at a coffee place in Nashville recently. I later saw one of the employees who works there. He wasn't working the day of the outreach, but when he came in the next day, our outreach was all the buzz. He was amazed at the attitude of some of the most resistant people in the restaurant. Some of the people he had been witnessing to for quite a while were the most intrigued at this outreach.

63 DOOR-TO-DOOR SUNDAY MORNING PAPER AND COFFEE
(3 PER TEAM)

THIS IS A SIMPLE project that will bring a smile to the face of your neighbors on Sunday mornings. Arrange for the delivery of several dozen copies of the local Sunday paper. Stack them on a dolly for easy transportation. In a couple of pots, carry some gourmet coffee—a regular and a decaf option. You may want to offer hot chocolate too.

Start at about 8:30 A.M., and stop at houses where newspapers haven't been delivered. Give those you visit a connection card.

WHERE TO GO
- Campuses
- Parks
- Neighborhoods
- Commuters

WHAT YOU'LL NEED
- □ Newspapers
- □ Insulated coffee pots (one coffee, one decaf, one hot chocolate)
- □ Cups
- □ Condiments
- □ Dolly (for carrying papers)
- □ Connection cards

64 FILTER CHANGE FOR AIR-CONDITIONERS AND HEATERS
(2 TO 3 PER TEAM)

HEATING AND AIR-CONDITIONING TECHNICIANS recommend that homeowners change their filters at least twice a year (spring and fall); some say once a month is even better. Go door to door with a variety of the common sizes of filters. Offer to install them for the owners.

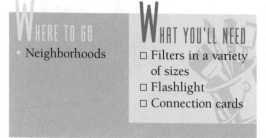

WHERE TO GO
- Neighborhoods

WHAT YOU'LL NEED
- ☐ Filters in a variety of sizes
- ☐ Flashlight
- ☐ Connection cards

This entire project usually takes five to ten minutes to pull off. Offer to pray for the homeowner as you leave. Leave a connection card.

65 GARAGE CLEANING
(3+ PER TEAM)

IT TAKES A LITTLE bit of courage to let someone clean and arrange your garage, but there are plenty of people who will take you up on this offer. Some are disabled, elderly, or overwhelmed with life and will welcome your offer. You might want to wear surgical filtering masks to prevent inhaling dust and other airborne particles.

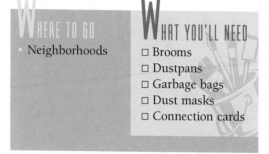

WHERE TO GO
- Neighborhoods

WHAT YOU'LL NEED
- ☐ Brooms
- ☐ Dustpans
- ☐ Garbage bags
- ☐ Dust masks
- ☐ Connection cards

Some garages are so bad they will be more than you can reasonably take on. Be willing either to say no or to come back with a larger team of workers. As with other projects, you don't want to overwhelm your people, and you don't want to get into something that can't be completed within two hours.

After you've cleaned someone's garage, you will know them fairly well. It will only be natural to offer to pray for them and to even invite them to your small group or church.

66 LEAF RAKING
(12 TO 20 PER TEAM)

EVERYBODY WANTS A HOUSE with mature trees in the yard. We write poems about the beauty of a tree, but those same people probably don't sing such a cheery song in the fall. With rakes in hand, go in teams from door to door and literally sweep through neighborhoods. This is a project that is best done with more than one group teaming up. Even a small yard with just a few people can be a bit overwhelming. Ideally, raking teams are made up of twelve to twenty high-energy members. With that number, you will make short work of someone's front yard.

Limit your offer to the front yard. Tell people up front, "Hi, we're showing God's love by raking the front yards of your neighborhood. You're next on the list!" Keep in mind the limited time and energy of your group when you make the offer. With the larger group, you will be able to knock off most yards in literally five minutes. It's something to behold when you get your team moving. The neighborhood will come outdoors just to watch!

To keep the momentum rolling with this, have someone going several houses ahead of the team to explain the project.

WHERE TO GO
• Neighborhoods

WHAT YOU'LL NEED
☐ Rakes
☐ Plastic leaf bags
☐ Connection cards

After the raking has been finished, have that same person stop back by the houses that have been served to say that you are done. At that time make the offer, "Is there anything we could pray about for you?"

On a practical note: If you have to bag the leaves, rake them into reasonably small piles. Designate some of your team as baggers. If you're fortunate enough to live in a community that vacuums the leaves from the curb, rake the leaves to the curb for the city to pick up.

IN ACTION: What about leaf blowers? We've tried them and actually have found they are not nearly as much fun as raking. Also, they don't allow as many to be involved in the team process, and they don't do as good a job at picking up all the leaves from the lawn. Stick to the good ol' tried-and-true rake.

67 LAWN MOWING
(5 TO 6 PER TEAM)

SEVERAL MOWERS DESCENDING ON a normal lawn is an awesome sight! Load several mowers into a pickup truck and drive around on spring and summer mornings looking for long grass. Often when the grass is long at a home, the people who live there have some sort of difficulty going on in their lives.

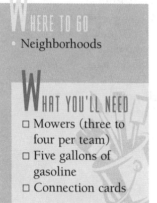

WHERE TO GO
- Neighborhoods

WHAT YOU'LL NEED
- ☐ Mowers (three to four per team)
- ☐ Five gallons of gasoline
- ☐ Connection cards

Unload the mowers from your truck and start them up as you knock on the door. That enthusiasm will positively impress those you are serving even as they open their front door. As they come to the door say, "We're doing a lawn mowing outreach in your neighborhood today for free—no donations—just to show you God's love in a practical way."

I recommend you confine your serving to mowing. When it comes to yard work, there's always more to do than you have time and resources for—raking up the grass, edging, hedge trimming, and so on.

IN ACTION: We have had some amazing stories come out of lawn care outreaches. Many of those we've served have opened up to us as we offered to pray for them. I recommend that as you serve in this way you look for open doors to more deeply intersect with people.

68 ROOF GUTTER CLEANING
(4 TO 5 PER TEAM)

WHERE TO GO
- Neighborhoods

WHAT YOU'LL NEED
- ☐ Ten-foot ladder
- ☐ Rubber gloves
- ☐ Plastic bags
- ☐ Connection cards

WHEN RAIN GUTTERS CLOG, they back up and begin to damage a house's roof. Just about every house needs an occasional gutter once-over. You will get pretty dirty on this one, so wear your old clothes.

Be watchful of bees and wasps. They love to make nests in eaves.

A pickup truck is helpful on this project, though not entirely necessary.

69 ADDRESS NUMBER PAINTING ON CURBS
(4 TO 5 PER TEAM)

MOST HOMEOWNERS WANT THEIR address nicely stenciled on their curbside. Go through the neighborhood a week in advance with a flyer explaining what you are doing and when you'll be coming by.

Even though not everyone in a neighborhood will want their number painted on the curb, they'll all hear about your offer of generosity.

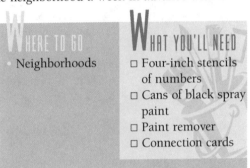

WHERE TO GO
- Neighborhoods

WHAT YOU'LL NEED
- ☐ Four-inch stencils of numbers
- ☐ Cans of black spray paint
- ☐ Paint remover
- ☐ Connection cards

70 GARBAGE CAN RETURN FROM STREET
(2 TO 3 PER TEAM)

THIS IS A PROJECT for early risers. Bring the empty cans up to the garage.

If you start to do this on a regular basis for your neighbors, I don't recommend you use a connection card each time. If those you are serving are your neighbors, the use of a card will feel a little stiff and formal. The first time you serve them, a card is okay to help them get the idea of why you are doing this. After that, I recommend you be a question answerer.

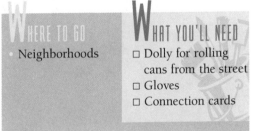

WHERE TO GO
- Neighborhoods

WHAT YOU'LL NEED
- ☐ Dolly for rolling cans from the street
- ☐ Gloves
- ☐ Connection cards

71 TULIP BULBS AND POTTED PLANTS
(3 TO 4 PER TEAM)

THIS IS A PROJECT that gives and keeps on giving each spring. Go door to door and offer to plant three to four tulip bulbs in the location of the homeowner's choosing. Next to the bulbs, place a laminated, weatherproof sign that reads, "Tulips Planted by _____ Church—Small Things Done with Great Love Will Change the World." Also include your church logo and phone number.

Do the same thing with potted plants. Mums and geraniums work well, and both are affordable when purchased in quantities.

Each year when the plants come up they'll remind the homeowners of the kindness shown them.

WHERE TO GO
- Campuses
- Parks
- Neighborhoods
- Downtown
- Shopping Centers

WHAT YOU'LL NEED
- ☐ Bulbs
- ☐ Plants
- ☐ Bulb digging tool (can be purchased at a nursery)
- ☐ Gloves
- ☐ Connection cards

IN ACTION: I ran into a woman just the other day who said, "You people gave me some mums two years ago. They are alive and healthy right by my front door. Just about every time I look at them I think of you people. Thanks so much." Some gifts just keep on giving.

72 SNOW REMOVAL FROM WALKS AND DRIVES
(5 TO 6 PER TEAM)

WHEN THE WEATHER IS horrible, you have a fantastic opportunity to show just how deep and wide the love of God flows in you to your community. When everyone else is inside battening down the hatches, your team can be out going the extra mile.

WHERE TO GO
- Neighborhoods

WHAT YOU'LL NEED
- ☐ Snow shovels
- ☐ Connection cards

Shovels work fine with this project. Snow blowers are quick and impressive, but can be dangerous.

73 ICE MELTING FOR SIDEWALKS
(3 to 4 per team)

THE CHEMICAL THAT MELTS ice from sidewalks is pretty inexpensive. After a hard freeze, a little sprinkled on the sidewalk can prevent a disaster. To do an ongoing "salt" outreach, first give out full one-gallon containers to homeowners with your group's name, logo, and phone number. (I suggest you don't use real salt, which can cause concrete to corrode; home supply centers stock a chemical "salt substitute" that doesn't harm pavement.)

After this initial outreach, return every few weeks and refill the bucket.

You'll need a dolly to transport the chemical (it's very heavy); a good supply of it (buy a lot before the season starts; it becomes hard to come by once the cold weather hits); scoops; and five-gallon buckets.

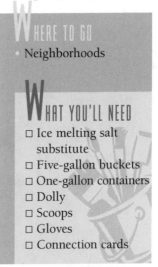

WHERE TO GO
- Neighborhoods

WHAT YOU'LL NEED
- ☐ Ice melting salt substitute
- ☐ Five-gallon buckets
- ☐ One-gallon containers
- ☐ Dolly
- ☐ Scoops
- ☐ Gloves
- ☐ Connection cards

74 WINDOW WASHING
(3 to 4 per team)

GO DOOR TO DOOR and offer to clean the outside windows of houses. This project is a lot of trouble for homeowners but is easy with the right equipment. To do the best job, go with the squeegees. If you are cleaning windows on a one-story house, you can get by with household window cleaner and paper towels.

WHERE TO GO
- Campuses
- Neighborhoods

WHAT YOU'LL NEED
- ☐ Squeegees (sold in auto supply stores, but I recommend higher quality brass versions sold at janitorial supply stores)
- ☐ Lamb's wool window scrubbers
- ☐ Rectangular plastic buckets (to fit the squeegees)
- ☐ Cleaning formula (available at janitorial supply stores)
- ☐ Eight-foot ladder
- ☐ Connection cards

75 LIGHT BULB REPLACEMENT
(3 TO 4 PER TEAM)

EVERYONE NEEDS LIGHT BULBS. Elderly or disabled people will be particularly grateful for this project. Knock on doors and offer the bulbs. You will no doubt hear the response, "We have bulbs already." A good reply is "But these are Christian light bulbs—they're free, like God's love!"

Offer to replace the bulbs for the homeowners. The most common bulbs are forty and sixty watts. These can be purchased at a deep discount for as little as a dime apiece. Put them in plastic bags with connection cards.

WHERE TO GO
- Campuses
- Neighborhoods
- Downtown

WHAT YOU'LL NEED
- ☐ Forty- and sixty-watt bulbs
- ☐ Six-foot ladder
- ☐ Canvas bags for carrying bulbs
- ☐ Connection cards

IN ACTION: A while back I did an outreach with several churches in the Dallas-Ft. Worth area. During our strategizing meeting, it was remarkable the diversity of people these leaders were interested in reaching out to—about every sector on the socioeconomic spectrum. But what sort of project would touch everyone? We ended up giving away light bulbs.

The project was a smashing success. Those in the lower middle class were happy to get a bulb for free. The elderly were grateful that someone was willing to install the bulbs for them. Even the wealthy who lived in a gated community gratefully received our free light bulbs. When they said, "But we already have light bulbs," our teams said, "Yes, but when was the last time you got a free one from Christians?"

76 FIREPLACE ASH REMOVAL
(3+ PER TEAM)

THIS IS A DIRTY job, but someone has to do it! In fact, it's one that many suburbanites need done. Go door to door with a small shovel, broom, and small dustpan. I don't recommend you use a vacuum cleaner. They create more problems than they solve. Stick to the brooms and dustpans.

Be careful not to get any hot ashes in your bag. This is dangerous due to fire and burn hazards.

Tie off the plastic bags that are full of ashes to avoid getting any on you. Put them directly in the trashcan when you're finished.

WHERE TO GO
- Neighborhoods

WHAT YOU'LL NEED
- ☐ Fireplace shovel
- ☐ Fireplace broom
- ☐ Plastic bags
- ☐ Dustpan
- ☐ Connection cards

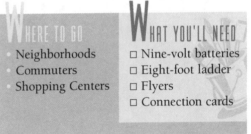

77 SMOKE DETECTOR BATTERY REPLACEMENT
(3+ PER TEAM)

FOR SAFETY, FIRE DEPARTMENTS encourage homeowners to change the nine-volt batteries in their smoke detectors on time change weekends each October and April. Spring into action on those weekends. Provide the battery, offer to change it, and leave a little reminder flyer that they should change their clocks that weekend too. The flyer should have your group or church's name, logo, and phone number listed.

WHERE TO GO
- Neighborhoods
- Commuters
- Shopping Centers

WHAT YOU'LL NEED
- ☐ Nine-volt batteries
- ☐ Eight-foot ladder
- ☐ Flyers
- ☐ Connection cards

As a couple of people are replacing the batteries, a designated evangelist needs to explain the point of your project.

78 LIBRARY FINES PAYMENT
(2 PER TEAM)

A PROJECT FOR THE quiet among you.

One way to do this is to give a ten-dollar bill to the librarian with the explanation, "I would like to pay the fines for the next several people who come in. I'll be sitting over at that table if anyone would like to talk to me."

You can also tell the librarian that you're going to pay the fines for the next hour, that you'll be sitting at the table off to the side,

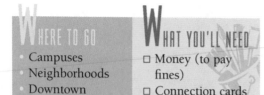

WHERE TO GO

- Campuses
- Neighborhoods
- Downtown

WHAT YOU'LL NEED

- ☐ Money (to pay fines)
- ☐ Connection cards

and that as soon as the next late book comes in to let you know.

IN ACTION: A rather shy woman at my church came up with this project. For some years, she has made it a point to do this outreach each time she goes to the library.

79 WINTER/SUMMER SURVIVAL KITS
(5 TO 10 PER TEAM)

WINTER CAN BE HARD on the body and the soul. A survival kit is a great encouragement to everyone who receives one.

The kit contains a packet of facial tissue, lip balm, and throat lozenges.

A similar kit for summertime includes lip balm, suntan lotion, moist towelettes, hard candy, and a connection card. The total cost of each of these is about one dollar.

WHERE TO GO

- Campuses
- Parks
- Neighborhoods
- Sporting Events
- Downtown
- Commuters
- Shopping Centers

WHAT YOU'LL NEED

- ☐ Zip-close plastic bags
- ☐ Lip balm
- ☐ Throat lozenges
- ☐ Individual packets of facial tissue
- ☐ Connection cards

IN ACTION: My church has had great success with this project as we've aimed it at parents and business professionals. We go to parks that parents frequent with their children. During the fall and winter months, we hit downtown sidewalks as business professionals make their way out to lunch. When those we meet notice how nice the kit is, they're very grateful and usually end up striking up a conversation with us.

80 CHRISTMAS TREE GIVEAWAY OR AFTER-CHRISTMAS TREE COLLECTION
(5 TO 10 PER TEAM)

SOME PEOPLE CAN'T AFFORD a tree, but a couple of days before the holiday, people in your small group or church can get them for free or just a few dollars per tree. Negotiate to get several dozen trees and get them with pickup trucks on about December 22. Drive through needy neighborhoods and give them out. A tactful way to do this is to knock on doors and say, "We're giving away Christmas trees to families who don't have one yet. Do you happen to know anyone who can't afford a tree this Christmas season?" If the person you're talking to needs one, he or she will speak up, or they can refer you to one of their neighbors. Usually the needy are well networked.

WHERE TO GO

- Campuses
- Parks
- Neighborhoods
- Downtown
- Commuters
- Shopping Centers

WHAT YOU'LL NEED

☐ Christmas trees
☐ Door hangers
☐ Truck
☐ Gloves
☐ Connection cards

In suburban neighborhoods, not many will need a free Christmas tree, but most will need to get rid of theirs a few days after Christmas. Put out door hangers the day after Christmas telling about your project and when specifically you will be coming around to collect the trees. Give the date and a time frame. The door hanger is great for connecting with the community because even if your services aren't used, your offer will have been made to a lot of people. Collect trees with a pickup truck and dump them at city-designated sites. Give all you serve a connection card.

81 LAUNDROMAT WASHER AND DRYER PAYMENT
(3 PER TEAM)

YOU MEET THE MOST interesting people in Laundromats! For this one you will need a supply of quarters, dimes, and laundry soap.

As people come in with their laundry, put the quarters into the machines and simply ask if they'd like cold, warm, or hot water. These startled people will likely think you are part of the laundry's staff, so you will have to tell them a couple of times you're Christians

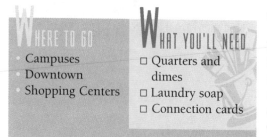
WHERE TO GO
- Campuses
- Downtown
- Shopping Centers

WHAT YOU'LL NEED
- ☐ Quarters and dimes
- ☐ Laundry soap
- ☐ Connection cards

and what you're doing.

Small-group members from my church have found that once they get into conversation with people, a sort of bonding takes place. Often, they're even invited to help fold clothes. That's pretty personal for someone you just met! We've found that people almost automatically ask us to pray for them. This is a fertile field for evangelism. Keep your eyes and ears open for opportunities.

82 COCOONS ON GOOD FRIDAY
(5 TO 10 PER TEAM)

TAKE THE IDEA OF the resurrection of Christ and turn it into powerful symbolism to use for an outreach project. For centuries, Christians have

WHERE TO GO
- Campuses
- Parks
- Neighborhoods
- Sporting Events
- Downtown
- Commuters
- Shopping Centers

WHAT YOU'LL NEED
- ☐ Cocoons
- ☐ Paper bags
- ☐ Special connection cards

likened the metamorphosis of the caterpillar into a butterfly to the death, burial, and resurrection of Christ. Our church has purchased cocoons over the Internet (www.butterflies.com) that were to hatch on Easter Sunday (they can be scheduled to hatch on a given day). We gave these out on Good Friday by the thousands to shoppers, business people, and others to take home to their families. We printed up a special connection card that explains how the resurrection of Christ is like the change of a caterpillar.

83 FRIENDLY PET OUTREACH TO CONVALESCENT AND RETIREMENT HOMES
(5 TO 10 PER TEAM)

AS A VETERAN OF the rehabilitation hospital scene, I know how depressing that atmosphere can be. Research has shown that physical contact with furry house pets can bring a lift to the spirit of patients.

Take two or three dogs (no cats!) to local homes and walk them on leashes from room to room to greet patients. It's amazing what a little tail wagging can do to lift a downcast attitude.

Not all dogs work well for this sort of ministry. Audition the potential dogs to find the laid back ones. Labradors are generally great visitation dogs. After our first visit, the patients usually know the dogs by name.

Bring a bag of treats for the patients to feed to the dogs while they pet them.

It's only natural to offer to pray for the patients while they are open-heartedly engaged in petting the dogs.

WHERE TO GO
- Neighborhoods
- Downtown

WHAT YOU'LL NEED
- ☐ Pets (calm ones that have been screened)
- ☐ Pet treats
- ☐ Connection cards

84 "FREE PRAYER" TABLE AT FAIRS
(5+ PER TEAM)

AT FAIRS, SWAP MEETS, bazaars, and grocery store exits you can find just about anything for sale from cheese to mousetraps to potpourri. Offer something much more helpful: prayer. Set up a table and a banner declaring your offer.

Either pray for people as they approach the table, or take prayer requests, which they fill out on special request cards and put in a box you have set up. If they want a follow-up call, you can arrange for that. Most will not want any sort of direct follow-up.

With this project, everyone on the team needs to be a designated evangelist. Have plenty of connection cards. Depending on the setting, be ready to field a wide variety of questions about the faith.

WHERE TO GO
- Campuses
- Sporting Events
- Downtown
- Shopping Centers

WHAT YOU'LL NEED
- ☐ Sign: "Free Prayer"
- ☐ Prayer request cards
- ☐ Pens
- ☐ Box
- ☐ Folding table/chairs
- ☐ Connection cards

IN ACTION: One church has had great success with the "free prayer" table approach at psychic fairs. They rent space at these events next to the palm readers, astrologers, and new agers of different sorts, and they simply offer to pray for people.

LEVEL 3
INVESTING IN THE CITY

ONCE YOU GET YOUR feet wet and have honed some evangelism skills, your group may be ready to jump in at the level of more thoroughly investing in the lives of your city. These projects are aimed at encountering people at the more difficult stress points of their lives. And they're designed to help your group get to know the needy of the city in a way that will allow you to begin to do something significant to meet their needs.

These projects are true investments in every sense of the word; they require more money and man-hours than blitzing or connecting projects. Because of this increased cost, it's a good idea to build momentum from blitzing to connecting before you involve yourself in the investing level of ministry.

One word of caution with these projects: Be careful what you promise. Many of those you are touching are used to being helped and are quick to interpret your offers for help as promises for more than you might be able to provide.

Investing projects are great for the following:

- *community building*
- a chance to *listen* deeply to the people of your city
- the greatest chance to *invite* people to your small group
- an opportunity to practice *praying* for people
- *building bridges* of credibility between you and the community

85 MATTHEW'S PARTY
(30+ NEEDED)

WHEN THE APOSTLE MATTHEW began to follow Christ, he was so enthusiastic he threw a big party, invited all his friends, and celebrated. Jesus and all the apostles attended and apparently had a great time (see Matthew 9:10). He was criticized for attending, eating, drinking—and with sinners! How scandalous! This was a great celebration that Matthew threw in honor of his newfound faith in the Messiah Jesus.

My church throws big parties in the spirit of what Matthew did. We fire up several barbeque grills and put on hot dogs and burgers. Multiple small groups provide desserts of all kinds. Kids' games with prizes abound. Local professional athletes make a showing. We've even raffled off a donated car (we gave the tickets away the day before and the day of the event; the winner had to be present to collect the prize).

After a couple of hours, more prayer, conversation, laughs, and hugs have happened than anyone can count. The neighborhood feels touched and invested in. Group members are invited into neighborhood homes. We've had close to a thousand guests show up to one of these bashes. Not only are the people of the neighborhood encouraged, loved, and prayed for, but also the members of the multiple small groups who sponsor it are built up by seeing their combined energies make a big impression.

IN ACTION: To see a Matthew's Party in action, check out our video on the web at www.kindness.com. Note: You will need Real Video software to view this. A free download is offered at the site.

WHERE TO GO

- Campuses
- Parks
- Neighborhoods
- Downtown

WHAT YOU'LL NEED

- ☐ Two banner signs (3x6 feet): "It's Party Time"
- ☐ Folding tables for serving (depending on how many you will serve)
- ☐ Coolers (several, depending on how many you will serve)
- ☐ Drinking cups
- ☐ Barbeque grills
- ☐ Burgers and hot dogs to grill
- ☐ Other food and beverages
- ☐ Ice
- ☐ Game centers for children (for example, face painting, balloon animals, penny toss)
- ☐ Connection cards

LEVEL 3

86 BLOCK PARTY
(12+ NEEDED)

MOST NEIGHBORS DON'T KNOW each other these days. Whether because of busyness or fear, there just isn't as much interaction

WHERE TO GO

- Campuses
- Parks
- Neighborhoods
- Downtown

WHAT YOU'LL NEED

☐ Grills
☐ Meats to grill
☐ Folding tables
☐ Drinks
☐ Ice
☐ Connection cards

within communities as there used to be. Yet most people are looking for ways to get to know each other. You can provide that in the form of a block party sponsored by your small groups.

Give the neighborhood a couple of weeks of notice. If the idea is original with your small group, use the name of the host family as the inviters. Divvy up the names of the neighborhood families as to who brings what food. Your group supplies the grills and the meat. To keep the time together fun, have some kids' activities such as a bicycle parade. Give prizes for the best decked-out bike. Have a raffle with a couple of small prizes. In advance of the dinner, talk with your group about the purpose of the event: to interact with the neighborhood as a group, not to interact strictly with one another as usual. In other words, focus out!

 IN ACTION: There are a lot of creative angles you can take with this project, depending on how complicated and large an event you want to stage. A group in Dayton does this project up in a big way by renting ponies for rides. Needless to say, they draw a lot of attention!

IN ACTION: A small group in a London suburb has done the community dinner project on a regular basis for several years. They've seen their city block turn from being a suspicious and isolated neighborhood to a downright neighborly place. The crime rate has actually gone down. Because the residents know each other better, they've begun to watch out for one another's property. The group has grown in numbers as it has been at the center of this neighborhood reformation.

87 LAMB'S LUNCH
(20+ PER TEAM)

HOMELESS PEOPLE NEED TO be loved, cared for, and shown that they are not forgotten. Often there's a great desire in the hearts of suburban

Christians to minister to homeless people. But there aren't a lot of safe opportunities for significant ministry. A Lamb's Lunch is a free hot meal served during the day, usually after a Sunday service, at an urban park. These events are staged in areas of town that would normally not be safe at night. But by day, in large groups of people, the risks are reasonable.

Serve a free hot meal for the homeless. Set up in a park with numbers of folding tables put end to end. Decorate the tables with cheery tablecloths.

The best foods are ones that are easy to serve in large quantity and easy to clean up afterward like spaghetti, sloppy joes, or lasagna. Be generous with your quantity of food. Our church has become famous among the homeless as the people who not only serve nice meals, but who also have the biggest and best meatballs with spaghetti! That's the kind of reputation you want.

WHERE TO GO
- Parks
- Downtown

WHAT YOU'LL NEED
- ☐ Folding tables
- ☐ Tablecloths
- ☐ Food to serve (we usually serve lasagna or spaghetti)
- ☐ Drinks
- ☐ Cups
- ☐ Ice
- ☐ Nice dessert
- ☐ Connection cards

LEVEL 3

IN ACTION: One group in the San Francisco area has combined the Lamb's Lunch with foot care for the homeless. They do blood pressure screening, wound care, and in particular they look after foot problems that are common to the homeless experience. Several registered nurses oversee a literal footwashing outreach to the men and women who congregate in an area park. Their outreach has saved the lives of several of the homeless who had gangrenous infections.

88 PARTIES OF APPRECIATION FOR POLICE OFFICERS, FIRE FIGHTERS, EMTs

THESE PUBLIC SERVANTS ARE constantly giving but typically go unthanked in their tasks. These wonderful people live very stressed-out lives. Their marriages suffer, they go for prolonged periods without sleep, and they often eat on the run. An occasional meal to serve the servants can make a big impression.

These people are going to be on call, so no matter how far in

WHERE TO GO
- Campuses
- Parks
- Neighborhoods
- Downtown

WHAT YOU'LL NEED
- ☐ Party supplies
- ☐ Thank-you card large enough for everyone in your group to sign
- ☐ Plenty of food (good food will be appreciated more than anything in this effort)
- ☐ Nametags

advance you plan, you'll have to be flexible according to emergencies that arise.

Arrange in advance to provide food. Agree before the outreach that your group will purposely spend time with the honorees and not with each other. Use nametags.

An alternative to a party is to provide a basket of fruit with a card of appreciation signed by each person in your church or group that explains how thankful you are for the lives and efforts of this crew.

89 ACCIDENT SCENE CLEANUP
(3+ PER TEAM)

IN THE WAKE OF traffic accidents, suicides, and acts of domestic violence, there are physical messes to clean up. But did you ever stop to wonder who does the dirty work after the public work is done? Usually, the very people who've done the emergency work are stuck with the unsavory cleanup tasks as well.

WHERE TO GO
- Campuses
- Parks
- Neighborhoods
- Downtown
- Commuters
- Shopping Centers

WHAT YOU'LL NEED
- ☐ Pager
- ☐ Cleanup caddy kit (window cleaner, porcelain cleaner, toilet cleaning brush, paper towels, rubber gloves)
- ☐ Connection cards

Approach the local police department first to explain what you want to do. To get a green light on this project, you'll need liability insurance coverage. Group coverage for liabilities of accidents that could occur during your outreaches is affordable. In addition, you might also have to sign a waiver with the local city government.

Once you've done the behind-the-scenes work, purchase supplies. Talk to the police and fire personnel for an accurate idea of what you'll need.

Set up an on-call system with a beeper. When an emergency

occurs, have team members available to take an assignment. The cleanup team should consist of three or more members at all times.

While there may not be a lot of opportunity to reach out to the people involved in the trauma, you will build some powerful connections with your local police force, EMTs, and other emergency personnel. You'll get a lot of questions along the lines of "Why in the world are you doing this?" As the apostle Peter encourages us, be ready to give an account of the hope that lies within you (see 1 Peter 3:15).

90 SINGLE PARENT'S HOUSE REPAIR
(3+ PER TEAM DEPENDING ON THE PROJECT)

THE CHALLENGES THAT COME with being a single parent are enormous. It goes with the territory when you combine raising kids, being a breadwinner, and not having enough hours in the day to do all that's needed.

WHERE TO GO
- Neighborhoods
- Downtown

WHAT YOU'LL NEED
- ☐ Tool kit (basic tools that fix-it people will have)
- ☐ Connection cards

You'll find this a gratifying and fruitful ministry to single parents by following a few simple rules:

Don't get into projects that you can't complete in two hours. As with other projects, two hours is about the maximum length that most volunteers can handle before a project moves from being enjoyable to being a burden.

Don't promise what you can't deliver. In some houses, almost everything will be broken. The laundry list of things that need to be fixed can get long fast. Prioritize by asking the homeowner, "Well, it looks like you have a lot that needs to be done. I have this much time with my team today. Which one or two things would you like us to put at the top of the list?" Then smile and go about your work. Realize that in some cases you could literally live in a house and never get done with all that needs to be fixed!

91 BLOOD PRESSURE SCREENING
(4+ PER TEAM)

HIGH BLOOD PRESSURE IS a serious health problem for millions of Americans. Contrary to popular myth, it affects people of all

WHERE TO GO

- Campuses
- Parks
- Neighborhoods
- Sporting Events
- Downtown
- Shopping Centers

WHAT YOU'LL NEED

- ☐ Blood pressure cups
- ☐ Stethoscopes
- ☐ Suckers (You enjoyed them when you visited the doctor as a kid, didn't you!)
- ☐ Connection cards

ages, walks of life, and ethnicity.

The actual taking of the blood pressure requires professionally trained nurses, but there's plenty of greeting and ushering other volunteers can do. Health care personnel will be familiar with the procedure; but for the rest of us, the general idea is this:

- Take the pressures. A typical blood pressure screening takes about five minutes.
- Direct those with hypertension (high blood pressure) to follow-up care. Those with very high blood pressure need to seek further medical attention immediately (essentially, dial 911).
- Issue a pocket card with the date and their pressure. (See our version of this card at www.servantevangelism.com.)

One of the beauties of this project is that it can be done in a variety of settings—fairs, bazaars, grocery stores, and so on. You might be rejected in your attempt to do outreach in certain settings. But take heart, you *will* get your foot in the door with this approach.

IN ACTION: Health professionals at my church are currently experimenting with other medical screenings including skin cancer, depression, blood sugar, and cholesterol. To get an update on what we are learning in these areas, check our website, www.servantevangelism.com.

IN ACTION: In New York City, a predominantly Filipino church tried repeatedly to connect with the residents of a high-rise apartment building. In spite of their shared ethnicity, they found every attempt to reach out thwarted until they connected on the basis of high blood pressure—a common problem among the residents. The net result of their outreach has been many fruitful conversations and prayer sessions after the blood pressure screenings. Now instead of one small group in that building, several meet there throughout the week.

92 TUTORING
(1 PER TEAM)

UNDERCLASSMEN SOMETIMES GET OFF to a rocky start when they make the transition from high school to college. Expectations on incoming college students are enough to intimidate even the most confident freshmen.

Advertise free tutoring throughout the campus. Team upperclassmen who are strong in a particular discipline with younger ones who are struggling. I suggest that teaming be same-sex to relieve any potential dating pressure. This also will prevent sexual harassment accusations or lawsuits.

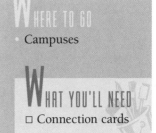

WHERE TO GO
• Campuses

WHAT YOU'LL NEED
☐ Connection cards

After the tutoring session, it is only natural to ask if it would be okay to pray with the students for success on their upcoming tests or projects. They'll almost always be open to that sort of prayer— usually they are fairly desperate! When the project comes back with a good grade, they have the beginning of a testimony of the faithfulness of God.

93 SCHOOL SUPPLIES FOR NEEDY FAMILIES
(10+ PER TEAM FOR DISTRIBUTING)

ONE KEY TO HELPING the outer reaches of your church provide ministry to the needy is to make it accessible by everyone—families included. Virtually everyone who attends your church is eager to give to needy people in some way. While they may not have the courage or time to get involved in something as involved as a Matthew's Party or a Lamb's Lunch, a school supply project in

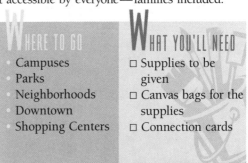

WHERE TO GO
• Campuses
• Parks
• Neighborhoods
• Downtown
• Shopping Centers

WHAT YOU'LL NEED
☐ Supplies to be given
☐ Canvas bags for the supplies
☐ Connection cards

the autumn is something families can do together. They can buy these supplies with their children so they learn what generosity is all about.

People from your church purchase school supplies for their children and a matching set for children of needy families at the same time. Issue a list of products you suggest they purchase for various grade levels.

94 DORM ROOM CLEANING
(4+ PER TEAM)

YOU WILL GET SOME attention with this project. Define what cleaning you'll be doing. Confine your offer to vacuuming and doing the windows. After cleaning, offer to pray for the students. When done, leave behind a bag of potpourri with your connection card attached.

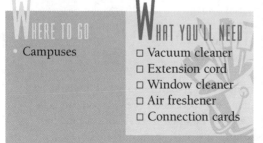

WHERE TO GO
- Campuses

WHAT YOU'LL NEED
- ☐ Vacuum cleaner
- ☐ Extension cord
- ☐ Window cleaner
- ☐ Air freshener
- ☐ Connection cards

Stop by a day in advance with a door hanger that advertises that your group will be coming through the area the following day (if it's Saturday morning, don't come before noon!). Carefully craft your door hanger so that it will become your connection card. Even if you don't end up cleaning all the rooms on the floor, you'll become known throughout the campus for your offer.

95 SHOPPING ASSISTANCE FOR SHUT-INS
(5+ PER TEAM)

AS BABY BOOMERS AGE, ministry to the physically disabled is guaranteed to be a growing topic.

Buy groceries, deliver them, put the groceries away (depending on how impaired the recipients are), and pray for the recipients.

Be careful what you promise—some of these residents will grow dependent on your project.

WHERE TO GO
- Neighborhoods

WHAT YOU'LL NEED
- ☐ Connection cards

A *caution:* Don't let this ministry fall on the shoulders of just one or two. Avoid the problem of compassion fatigue. Share this ministry as a group. Be clear up front that you will be able to help for a given time—say, for a month.

96 APARTMENT MOVE-OUT HELP
(5+ PER TEAM)

MOVING OUT OF AN apartment is a miserable job. With a little bit of cleaning equipment and some availability, your team can make short work of this chore. This project requires a team of five or more to avoid overwhelming the cleaners.

WHERE TO GO
• Neighborhoods
• Downtown

WHAT YOU'LL NEED
☐ Vacuum cleaners
☐ Carpet deodorizer
☐ Extension cords
☐ Broom and dustpan
☐ Window cleaner
☐ Bathroom cleaner
☐ Paper towels or rags
☐ Air freshener
☐ Trash bags
☐ Connection cards

Contact the apartment management and explain your project vision. Once you've gained favor with management, you'll have plenty of opportunities handed to you in the future.

You'll need a couple of vacuum cleaners, a quantity of trash bags, a bathroom cleaning kit, and some connection cards. To make this a bit more of a party, order pizza toward the end of your cleaning session.

After cleaning and finishing up any packing, it will be only natural to offer to pray for those you've been serving.

Also, keep in mind that most of those you are serving are people moving out of one living situation to another. They likely are not leaving the area, so your act of kindness will bear fruit locally.

97 BIRTHDAY PARTY ORGANIZING
(5+ PER TEAM)

SOME PEOPLE WON'T EVER have a birthday party unless you organize it for them. In my years of doing servant evangelism, I've been amazed at the number of times people have offhandedly remarked, "You know, today is my birthday. This little expression of love that you have shown me is the only gift I received today. Thanks!" There are a lot of lonely,

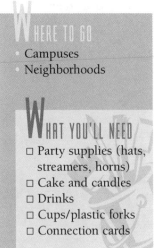

WHERE TO GO
- Campuses
- Neighborhoods

WHAT YOU'LL NEED
- ☐ Party supplies (hats, streamers, horns)
- ☐ Cake and candles
- ☐ Drinks
- ☐ Cups/plastic forks
- ☐ Connection cards

forgotten people in your community.

Convalescent homes are an especially good place to do parties. Some of these residents have been virtually abandoned by their families. A little attention to these forgotten people will make a big impression.

I recommend designing your party to include children, pets, and a cake to celebrate everyone whose birthday occurred that week or month.

I've found that a key to making this project work is finding some party people — those who have the gift for making a party happen. Let your hospitality people shine in this setting.

98 MEMORIAL SERVICE FOR THE UNCHURCHED
(6+ PER TEAM)

WHERE DO THE UNCHURCHED turn when it comes to death and dying?

This idea may seem like a bit of a paradigm shift for some. Most church systems are used to paid pastors doing the professional work

WHERE TO GO
- Neighborhoods

WHAT YOU'LL NEED
- ☐ Connection cards

of the ministry, while the lay people do some nonprofessional parts of ministry (at best). Why not allow gifted teams of lay people to do comprehensive care for those going through the grieving process — including caring for the family and even speaking at the memorial service. While this idea may not be possible in your current tradition, it's an idea worth pondering.

As a veteran of twenty years of pastoral ministry, I'll let you in on a secret: It doesn't take an ordained minister to perform a memorial service. The primary gifts required to do this (not including a heavy dose of courage) are a little ability to speak, some compassion, and a heart to listen. To demystify this a bit further, those attending a memorial service don't need to hear a lengthy sermon or a beautifully honed, three-point, completely original message. They need to hear that there is more to life than the physical dimension. Set up a meal for attendees after the service.

Extend this idea further by serving as volunteer chaplains, working with your small group to bring comfort to families facing a time of loss. Coordinate this with the professional ministry staff at your church. Some of the best caregivers and grief-assisters are from the ranks of lay people. When a small group has provided prayer and other support to a family during a death and dying process, it also makes sense that the pastoral care process continue through to a memorial service.

As a group, get involved with the obvious needs of providing for the family in the areas of food, prayer, and encouragement. More importantly, in the weeks after the loss, remain in contact with the family. Make it clear that they are still in your prayers. Ask them if there is anything specific that can be done for them by the group. Offer to provide meals in the weeks that follow.

Take out an ad in the paper: "Don't have a church? Memorial services provided free of charge."

And when people call in, offer this public service.

99 MOVE-IN WELCOMING PARTY
(5+ PER TEAM)

THE GOAL OF THIS project is to quickly make a positive impression on new neighbors. As Welcome Wagon winds down in popularity in many cities, this opportunity becomes a better one. On move-in day, new residents never seem to have enough help — regardless of how many friends they have. Contact the management of apartment buildings with your plan. Explain that you're part of the welcoming crew — complete with a first meal for the new residents. Once they see that you're for real, they'll call you when new people move into their complex.

Provide the first meal. Pizza is something nearly everyone loves. Stock up on items new tenants might have forgotten: shelf paper, carpet deodorizer, light bulbs.

WHERE TO GO

- Neighborhoods

WHAT YOU'LL NEED

- ☐ Pizza
- ☐ Drinks
- ☐ Cups and napkins
- ☐ Ice
- ☐ Greeting card
- ☐ Connection cards

100 POOL PARTY WITH A PURPOSE!
(10+ DEPENDING ON THE SIZE OF YOUR PARTY)

SWIMMING POOLS ARE GREAT connecting places for casual conversation. Those who don't yet know the Lord will sometimes say yes to an invitation to a pool when they wouldn't come directly to a church or a small group.

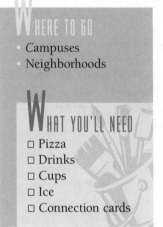

WHERE TO GO
- Campuses
- Neighborhoods

WHAT YOU'LL NEED
- ☐ Pizza
- ☐ Drinks
- ☐ Cups
- ☐ Ice
- ☐ Connection cards

Invite two nonChristians for every one person in your group.

The key to making this project work is talking with your group in advance to make sure they understand why you're doing this project. It's all about connecting with the guests you've invited. On the day of the event, a couple of people need to take leadership to keep this focus going during the event or the Christians will naturally congregate with one another, get into God talk, and forget about the purpose of the party. Avoid that temptation! This is an outwardly focused party.

At the end of the party, spend a few minutes with someone from your group giving a testimony. Don't make it too long—literally five minutes is plenty. This testimony needs to be tightly scripted with these elements:

- the person's story
- how he or she met Christ
- the difference Christ has made in his or her life

Five minutes is not long, but it's about as long as a group can sit still and not feel they are being held captive.

I wouldn't try to "close the deal" with them spiritually at this time. Have group members hang around for dessert and coffee after the testimony. You may find the JESUS video helpful to give out as a follow-up tool. (For information on the JESUS video, go to *www.campuscrusade.com,* or call 1-800-827-2788.)

101 BIRTHDAY CARDS
(2+ PER TEAM)

SIMPLE THINGS DONE FAITHFULLY can make a big impression on people. Several years ago I began a personal ministry of sending birthday cards to many who would have otherwise been forgotten, and now I send several hundred a year. Many people tell me that mine is the only one they receive each year.

Something as small as a birthday card can open doors to the Holy Spirit's power. There are people living very near you or your group who will not receive a birthday card this year. You could begin a new ministry by doing a simple survey of the neighborhood. Begin by knocking on doors and saying, "Hi, I'm ___, your neighbor a few doors down [if you haven't met yet]. I think everyone should receive a birthday card each year. So if you wouldn't mind, my small group that meets each week at my house would like to send you one." You'll find people a bit surprised, but also very open to your invitation. Probably no one has ever asked them for their birthdate for a good reason! This connection will likely open doors for you and your group to approach these neighbors later when other needs come up.

WHERE TO GO

- Campuses
- Neighborhoods

WHAT YOU'LL NEED

□ Birthday cards
□ Connection cards

WHAT TO SAY

"FREE!"
Don't take any money for any of your projects, even if it is offered. To receive money robs the gift you're giving of its power.

Free is a powerful, stimulating word to modern people. It is both disarming and gratifying at the same time. I can't tell you how many people I've heard say over the years, "No one has ever given me anything free in my life." I suspect for each person who has verbalized that sentiment, there are numbers more who have thought it. In this day of the you-don't-get-anything-for-free-anymore mentality, giving people something for free is truly unusual.

"WE'RE DOING A COMMUNITY SERVICE PROJECT!"
With this little phrase, you give people a bit of context for the sort of project you're doing. In their minds you're not so different from the Kiwanis, Boy Scouts, or other community groups. Of course, you're doing your outreach project with a completely different motivation from the other groups'. It's okay to give people a familiar context that makes sense on their terms.

"WE'RE HERE SHOWING GOD'S LOVE IN A PRACTICAL WAY!"
When you're out serving, there is always a question of "how much should we say to people when we are serving?" and "what should we say to people when we are serving?" I've found that the little phrase above has enough content that the average person will understand.

"WE'RE CHRISTIANS."
It's a mistake to push your church's name too much. On the one hand, we'd love to see people find their way into our church. On the other hand, we don't want to come across as self-promotional. If those you serve sense that you're there to grow your membership roster, they'll be turned off. Bear in mind, unchurched people are far more sensitive to self-promotion than most Christians.

The connection card has plenty of specific information for people to follow-up on if they want to. My experience is that as you serve with the right motive, people will spontaneously ask questions about your church without you forcing the issue. Your group will grow as you begin to live with an outward focus. Making more of your church name than is necessary is a mistake.

"IF JESUS WERE IN TOWN, WE THINK HE'D BE SAYING THINGS, BUT HE'D ALSO BE DOING THINGS FOR PEOPLE."

This explanation seems to make the most sense to unchurched people. In response to the question, "What would Jesus do?" the unchurched seem to think he'd be very practical in his expression of love. They often say in response to this explanation, "I always thought that if Jesus were to come to my city he'd be doing things like this." You'll touch something intuitive in people when you touch their hearts through acts of generosity and kindness.

TEN BEST PROJECTS TO GET YOU STARTED

WHEN YOU FIRST LAUNCH the idea of servant evangelism, the primary goal is to have a successful experience for your group. You want your group members to come back from their time together with a gung-ho attitude and to say, "We had a great time. Let's do this again—soon!" You want participants to enjoy themselves so much they'll not only come back the next time you do an outreach project, they'll also want to bring their friends.

1. **TOTALLY FREE CAR WASH (SEE PAGES 61-63)**
   If you're just starting out with servant evangelism and the weather permits, this is a good place to begin. Though not a high-volume project, it's a great starting place for seeing the power of kindness touch the human heart.

   A car wash costs essentially nothing to do. There is something for everyone here, including children. Get plenty of signs. Find a good location with a lot of cars driving past. Put some enthusiastic cheerleaders out on the street with your signs, and go for it. Don't forget to have a designated evangelist who explains to the recipients what is going on.

2. **SOFT DRINK GIVEAWAY (SEE PAGES 27-29)**
   If you want to do a little more investing in product and to touch a larger group, this is probably the way to go. Set up at a stop light. The police probably won't mind your outreach as long as you're mindful of the flow of traffic when the light changes.

   Try to give away at least two hundred drinks on your first outing, even if you are a small group. You'll be surprised how fast that many drinks will go. Get plenty of cards printed. What you don't use the first time out, you can use later.

3. **CHRISTMAS GIFT-WRAPPING (SEE PAGES 77-78)**
   If you've gotten your feet wet doing a project or two and you want to step out a bit further for Christmas, gift-wrapping is wonderful. You will attract a lot of attention among shoppers. Be ready for a possible onslaught of business. Be careful what you promise to the store management on your first time out

with this. If the total workforce is your one small group, I suggest you sign up for just one weekend before Christmas.

We've found that malls are also open to the idea of gift-wrapping at Valentine's Day, Mother's Day, and other gift-buying holidays.

4. LEAF RAKING (SEE PAGE 81)

As the saying goes, there's safety in numbers. When it comes to serving, this is a slam dunk. Find the yards in your part of town that have a lot of leaves, and go for it. Just make sure you have enough rakers on your team so that no one gets worn out.

5. BUSINESS BLAST (SEE PAGES 40-41)

If you're coming up on one of the special days mentioned (page 41), pick up candy or flowers and serve the servants. You may be surprised how open-hearted they are when the tables are turned and you're on the giving end.

6. NEWSPAPER GIVEAWAY (SEE PAGES 37-38)

Your mother always said, "Don't play in traffic." She was partly right. Just don't go into traffic with your newspapers when the light is green. Set up on a busy corner and give away your papers at the red light.

7. BIRTHDAY PARTY ORGANIZING AT A NURSING HOME (SEE PAGES 101-102)

There are few places where your kindness will be more appreciated than the local nursing home. For many, this gesture will be the first time they've been remembered in years. Know that in touching the one you focus on, you are not reaching out to the one resident, but to the extended family, who will surely hear about your act of kindness.

8. GROCERY BAG PACKING (SEE PAGES 41-42)

Most people need their groceries bagged. Find one of the big discount grocers and approach the manager with your idea. This is a great project because it can be done any day of the year, regardless of weather conditions.

9. GIVEAWAYS (SEE PAGES 31-32)

Once you've explained to a store manager your vision for serving the city and gotten in on his good graces, you have a powerful outreach location for the future.

Situate yourselves at the entrance, not the exit, of the store. On the way out of the store, customers are in a hurry to get out to their cars. They won't take what you have, and your servant team members will feel rejected.

10. TWENTY-DOLLAR OUTREACH EXPERIMENT (SEE PAGES 36-37)
For a little investment of money, your group will learn a lot with this project. This is a great way to jumpstart your group into the ministry of servant evangelism. If your people are a little shy, team up in groups of two or three. The ideas don't have to be completely original. Try one of the many ideas outlined in this book. If you get another idea, that's even better. Don't forget to celebrate the projects that are the most daring, most creative, touched the most people, and so on.

TOP 10 WORST OUTREACH IDEAS

WHILE MOST OF THE projects we've tried over the years in the name of servant evangelism have worked well, a few have failed. In fact, some have blown up in our faces. When I tell story after story of successful outreach ventures, it can sound like everything we touch in the world of outreach automatically turns to gold. It's just not so! I thought you might be encouraged in your creativity when you see how ours have backfired on occasion.

Each of these ideas seemed like a good one during our planning meeting before the outreach. Somehow we just didn't think the details through thoroughly enough. I share these projects with you in hope that you will not try these with your small group.

(Okay, this is a made-up list. So, seriously, don't try any of these projects. I repeat—all are very poor outreach ideas.)

10. Free mainframe computer maintenance service
9. Caramel apple giveaway at orthodontist's office
8. Match giveaway at Smokers Cessation Seminar
7. Coke giveaway on the interstate
6. Free pet embalming
5. In-mouth denture cleaning at rest homes
4. Toga giveaway on campus of Oral Roberts University
3. Car wash in Amish country
2. Urinal cleaning during half-time at professional football games
1. Three words: Free Body Piercing

ABOUT THE AUTHOR

STEVE SJOGREN (pronounced "shów grin") is the founding pastor of the Vineyard Community Church in Cincinnati, Ohio, which has six thousand weekend attendees. He is the pioneer of the concept of servant evangelism—the simple, straightforward approach to outreach outlined in *101 Ways to Reach Your Community*. His first book, *Conspiracy of Kindness* (Vine Books, Ann Arbor, MI, 1993), has sold 100,000 copies worldwide and has spawned a movement of outward-focused church life.

To check out new projects and to be linked with other groups around the world that are doing servant evangelism, check out the website, *www.servantevangelism.com*, or call 1-888-KINDNESS.